Creepy
CALIFORNIA

Creepy CALIFORNIA

STRANGE *and* GOTHIC TALES *from the* GOLDEN STATE

KEVEN MCQUEEN

AN IMPRINT OF
INDIANA UNIVERSITY PRESS
BLOOMINGTON AND INDIANAPOLIS

This book is a publication of

Quarry Books an imprint of
INDIANA UNIVERSITY PRESS

Office of Scholarly Publishing
Herman B Wells Library 350
1320 East 10th Street
Bloomington, Indiana 47405 USA

iupress.indiana.edu

© 2017 by Keven McQueen
All rights reserved

No part of this book may be reproduced or utilized in any form or by any means, electronic or mechanical, including photocopying and recording, or by any information storage and retrieval system, without permission in writing from the publisher. The Association of American University Presses' Resolution on Permissions constitutes the only exception to this prohibition.

The paper used in this publication meets the minimum requirements of the American National Standard for Information Sciences—Permanence of Paper for Printed Library Materials, ANSI Z39.48–1992.

Manufactured in the United States of America

Library of Congress Cataloging-in-Publication Data

Names: McQueen, Keven, author.
Title: Creepy California : strange and Gothic tales from the Golden State / Keven McQueen.
Description: 1st [edition]. | Bloomington : Indiana University Press, 2017. | Includes bibliographical references.
Identifiers: LCCN 2017011846 (print) | LCCN 2017024182 (ebook) | ISBN 9780253029133 (e-book) | ISBN 9780253029058 (pbk. : alk. paper) | ISBN 9780253028914 (cloth : alk. paper)
Subjects: LCSH: Haunted places—California. | Ghosts—California. | Curiosities and wonders—California. | Tales—California. | Legends—California. | Folklore—California.
Classification: LCC BF1472.U6 (ebook) | LCC BF1472.U6 M433 2017 (print) | DDC 398.209794—dc23
LC record available at https://lccn.loc.gov/2017011846

1 2 3 4 5   22 21 20 19 18 17

Dedicated to some of my favorite Californians:
Jo Blanset; Carlton Grizzle; author Thomas S. Fiske;
and Ben Eshbach and Kiara Geller of
that great band The Sugarplastic.

Note to the reader:
For maximum effect, read this book aloud
in a Boris Karloff voice.

CONTENTS

	Acknowledgments	ix
	Introduction	xi
1	Tales from the Tombs	1
2	Eight Million Peculiar Ways to Die	14
3	Strange Circumstances	28
4	Otherworldly Wise: Coastal Ghosts	37
5	Predators and Prey: True Crime Stories	42
	Bibliography	117

ACKNOWLEDGMENTS

They assisted:

Drema Colangelo; Eastern Kentucky University Department of English; Eastern Kentucky University Interlibrary Loan Department (Stefanie Brooks, Heather Frith, Shelby Wills); Amy McQueen and Quentin Hawkins; Darrell and Swecia McQueen; Darren, Alison, and Elizabeth McQueen; Kyle McQueen; Michael, Lori, and Blaine McQueen and Evan Holbrook; Ashley Runyon and everyone at the Indiana University Press; and Mia Temple. Also: the Mediator.

INTRODUCTION

THERE ARE MANY GUIDEBOOKS TO CALIFORNIA THAT inform tourists about the state's justly famous wonders, but the information in these books is incomplete. For example, we hear about the wonderful Sequoia National Forest. But regarding the subject of California's trees, why do we never hear about the lonesome Fort Bragg resident who carved a family for himself out of wood?

California is proud of its movie industry, but the guidebooks neglect to tell us about the ten-year Hollywood conspiracy, which included actress Carole Lombard, to spare an elderly woman from learning that her son had died in a bizarre shooting accident.

We are familiar with the state's many first-rate institutions of higher learning, yet the topic of Stanford's secret collection of occult memorabilia never seems to come up.

California guidebooks that want to give readers an impression of the residents' personality mention the individualistic streak—some would say downright eccentricity—of many Golden Staters, which has become a national cliché. However, the guidebooks are softballing matters. As far back as 1888, a mental health expert predicted California would be entirely populated by lunatics within twenty years or so.

This book includes all of these true stories and many more, thereby exploring a side of the state that guidebooks dare not mention. Never mind the scenery, the beaches, and the ideal weather; this is the California that is home to bizarre epitaphs, giant skeletons, unsolved murders, persons who kept embalmed bodies in their homes, serial killers, peculiar suicides, and grave robberies—including a case in which the deceased's mistress had his body secretly exhumed and reburied to spite his widow. Strangely, the Beach Boys didn't mention any of these things in their songs!

Creepy
CALIFORNIA

1
TALES FROM THE TOMBS

Live Burial

A HORRIFYING CASE OF *INTENTIONAL* LIVE BURIAL occurred at Hat Creek in March 1921. William T. of the Hat Creek Indian tribe died of smallpox and was placed in a coffin, which two fellow tribesmen bore to his grave in the dark of night. But it seems he was not incurably dead; the pallbearers heard him kicking the lid but buried the coffin anyway, fearing the wrath of the health officer. Chief Samson brought the matter to the proper authorities' attention.

Tombstone Talk

A pioneer-era tombstone allegedly in Grass Valley bears this epitaph: "Lynched by mistake. The joke's on us."

On Supreme Court Justice Silas Sanderson's headstone, Laurel Hill Cemetery, San Francisco: "Final decree."

On a headstone in Welwood Murray Cemetery, Palm Springs: "Louisa Adler, 1873–1933. Died of grief caused by a neighbor. Now rests in peace."

On the headstone of TV game show producer Merv Griffin, Westwood Memorial Park, Los Angeles: "I will not be right back after this message."

On actress Joan Hackett's headstone, Hollywood Forever Cemetery, Los Angeles: "Go away—I'm asleep."

Will Power

Robert D., a wealthy landowner of Chico, died on October 22, 1871. He had a reputation for eccentricity, and the terms of his will did nothing to lessen that impression. Robert left $100,000 to the Deaf and Dumb Asylum at San Francisco because, as he told friends, "I want to leave it to those who will not talk about me after I am dead."

Louise W. of Los Angeles was disappointed when one of her daughters moved to France to live a sinful existence. Louise's bitterness was reflected in her will, which was filed on May 29, 1912: "To my daughter, Edith, living in the Champs-Élysées, Paris, I bequeath $5 with which she must purchase the work of a reliable author on the wages of sin and ingratitude."

Annie P. of Los Angeles died on May 11, 1933. She adored her pet parrot so much that she couldn't bear the thought of being parted from it. Apparently, she thought the parrot felt the same way because her will directed that the bird be euthanized painlessly via chloroform and buried with her. Mistress and parrot began the Long Journey together on May 15.

―·―◦―·―

Margaret K. was an avowed hermit and a man-hater. The daughter of a Utah silver magnate, she lived practically alone in a $100,000 (equal to over $1 million in modern currency) Palos Verdes mansion with a magnificent hilltop view of the ocean; it also had barred gates and was surrounded by a twelve-foot wall. Margaret had only one servant, and she gave him instructions via telephone or written note rather than interact with him in person. On the rare occasions when she left the house, she was heavily veiled. Neighbors called her "the mystery woman of Palos Verdes."

Margaret committed suicide by anesthetic on April 28, 1933, at age forty-nine, in a second mansion she owned in Beverly Hills. She left a note: "I don't want to live if I can't see the beautiful trees and the sea. I'm losing my sight, so I've decided to shove off. Please don't let busybodies into my house."

Strange as Margaret's life was, she was even stranger after death. In accordance with her wishes, her funeral consisted of a three-day classical music concert. A news report stated, "No one but a woman attendant was permitted to look on the body in the seventy-two hours it lay in state. The orchestra played in an adjoining chapel. Flowers about the bier were changed regularly. The funeral clothes were changed daily." At the end of the third day, her body was cremated and the ashes scattered.

In December, as relatives battled over Margaret's money, her brother-in-law Paul W. claimed that the woman who had said "I hate all humans, especially men" once gave him $300 after he kissed her. "Instead of being mad, as I half expected, she smiled all over," he declared. So maybe she liked *one* person.

Embalmed for the Ages

A woman died in San Francisco in 1881, after which the undertaker embalmed her and placed her hermetically sealed coffin in his basement awaiting further instructions as to the dispensation of the remains. Those instructions never came, and the mortician forgot about the body in the cellar until December 1888, when the new owner of the establishment found the neglected merchandise. A check into the deceased's background showed that the woman had actually played a role in one of the most notorious unsolved crimes of the century: she was the so-called daughter of Emma Cunningham, who had been tried for—and acquitted of—knifing to death her former lover, dentist Harvey Burdell, in New York City in 1857. The woman in question wasn't the actual child of Emma but rather the baby of a pauper woman whom Emma had tried to pass off as the fruit of an obviously bogus "secret marriage" between herself and the notoriously misogynistic bachelor dentist. (The reader can find the entire absurd tale in Jack Finney's 1983 book *Forgotten News*.) The ersatz offspring of Emma and the doctor had, ironically, married a dentist for real.

Liora T., elderly and eccentric, ended her earthly career in her cottage in Boyle Heights, Los Angeles, in November 1905. Neighbors thought she lived entirely alone, but that was a mistake. In her storeroom was a hermetically sealed three-foot box hidden under a mound of garbage. An engraved silver plate was nailed to the lid: "Liora. Died December 16, 1877. Aged 27 years, 2 months, 1 day."

When the box was opened, it was found to contain the dismembered remains of Liora's daughter, who had died back East on the date inscribed on the plate. There was also a disinterment certificate dated November 7, 1881, and signed by an undertaker in Amherst, Massachusetts.

Nanette and Mary, unmarried sisters, moved to Los Angeles from Toledo in 1912. They lived in the same apartment and became notorious for their secrecy.

With the dawning of 1914, neighbors noticed something about the sisters' apartment: boy, did it reek! And the smell got more robust every day. On January 30, the police investigated the stench and found a raving Nanette sitting beside the body of Mary, who had died three weeks previously. The mystery of the stink was solved.

Not surprisingly, Nanette was carted off to the insane asylum for observation. One of her few lucid comments was "I do like violets."

As an interesting sidelight, the sisters' father, Samuel, a retired buggy and wagon manufacturer, had disappeared without a trace from Toledo in 1878. His vanishing was called "one of the most impenetrable mysteries in police annals."

Alice S. of Long Beach had a unique item for sale: the petrified remains of her son, Theron. He had died at Imperial on April 18, 1923, at age twenty; five years later he was exhumed from an El Centro cemetery for removal to another resting place and was found to be an unusually stiff stiff. A physician who examined the body thought young Theron had achieved his toughened state not through petrifaction but due to excessive embalming fluid.

Alice—knowing a good business opportunity when she saw one—convinced elderly John, a railroad engineer of Meridian, Mississippi, to invest his life's savings of $32,000 in a scheme to sell the petrified body to scientists for prices ranging from a respectable $25,000 to an awe-inspiring $350,000.

The riches were not forthcoming, and John took Alice to court for fraud in December 1928; he had her letters to enter as evidence. She came to court on a stretcher, claiming to be suffering from influenza. Doctors said she was shamming.

On December 22, a jury found Alice guilty on five counts of using the mail to defraud John. She faced a total of twenty-five years in prison.

Cemetery Duel

John, a San Francisco fireman, fought a duel with an unnamed man on September 14, 1878. Two circumstances made the fight unique. In a typical duel, combatants stood firm a certain distance apart and the contest was considered over after they fired once at each other, whether hit or miss; John and his enemy, however, advanced upon each other, firing as they went. Also, the duel was held in the middle of a Catholic cemetery. Both men were injured, John near the heart.

Robbing Graves, Snatching Bodies

In October 1878, an unknown man shot himself in the forehead on Long Wharf in Oakland. The coroner kept the body at the morgue, but when no relatives claimed it, it was buried in the potter's field section of Mountain View Cemetery.

Soon, three men asked the coroner if the man he had recently buried had a distinctive tattoo on his right forearm. The coroner confirmed it and showed the men a ring worn by the suicide. The men said the dead man was their brother and requested that the body be exhumed so they could bury it in the family cemetery.

The coroner directed James, the man in charge of burying paupers, to exhume the brother. The dead man's brothers noticed that James dragged his feet and was reluctant to do his job. Even when the coffin was unearthed, James refused to open it and seemed to wish he was somewhere else. The brothers found out why after a workman pried the lid open: the suicide was laid to rest stripped of his clothing, beheaded, and "bearing the marks of the most frightful butchery."

James had some fast talking to do. He admitted that he had cut off the brother's head and sold it to a doctor for six bucks without the coroner's knowledge. As for the fine new clothes, James had been wearing them whenever he went out on the town and wished to impress the ladies. The doctor, fortunately, was a sport and sewed the corpse's head—which he had preserved in a jar of alcohol—back onto the body, good as new (in a manner of speaking). The brother got the decent burial he deserved, and James got the trouble he deserved.

On Memorial Day 1924, crowds of the thoughtful entered Sacramento's Eastlawn Cemetery to pay tribute to Those Who Came Before Us. They found that a tomb had been burgled during the night. The victim of this "victimless crime" was Alex, who was king of the gypsy tribes in the United States until death unseated him from his throne in 1917. Someone had believed the rumor that gypsy chieftains are buried with valuables and decided to see for himself—no word as to whether the ghoul emerged the richer from his labors.

Fighting Over Elias

Elias Lipsis had a famous sister, Adah Issacs Menken, a world-renowned actress more noted for her flesh-colored tights and scandalous affairs than for her histrionic skills. Elias became stage manager of the Bella Union Theater in San Francisco. His marriage to actress Carrie W. was not happy; she suspected—with good cause—that he was an adulterer. On May 2, 1879, Elias shot at his wife during an argument. Fortunately, he missed. The couple kissed and made up, but fear of being convicted for attempted murder led Elias to choose annihilation. On May 3, he shot himself in the presence of his wife.

In August, Carrie went to Laurel Hill Cemetery to place flowers on her husband's grave and was miffed to find that a strange, and very pretty, younger woman was already there arranging a floral cross.

"Who are you, and why are you putting flowers on my darling Elias's tomb?" demanded the widow (or words to that effect).

"I am Rose," sniffed the other. "And Elias loved me *much* more than his wife!"

A violent argument followed in which neither woman comported herself with much dignity and each accused the other of driving Elias to a suicide's grave. The widow claimed that only *she* had the right to decorate her husband's patch of turf and nourish it with her tears. Rose disagreed, and she triumphantly showed Carrie a letter that Elias had written to her, dated April 9, which she just happened to have with her:

> I am not in the best of spirits, for my *wife* arrived this noon from Virginia City, and I have had hell. Now, my darling, don't for God's sake think less of me on account of her returning, for I swear to you, my darling, that I love only you, and to lose you would break my heart. Don't think me foolish for writing in this manner. These are the true sentiments of my heart.

That made the widow livid. A few days later, she had even greater reason to be furious: rumor held that Rose—who, as the *Police Gazette* said, was "tired of the necessity of timing her weeping to suit the convenience of Carrie"—had bribed someone to remove Elias from his grave and bury him in a different section of the cemetery—a place where Rose grieved secretly and gloated at her victory over Carrie. If the story was true, Carrie had been mourning at an empty tomb!

The matter of the unauthorized exhumation was brought to cemetery superintendent Eugene D., who, according to the *San Francisco Post*, "pooh-poohed the matter and tried to laugh it down." His laughter, it would later be proved, was of the nervous variety. A detective insisted that Elias's official grave be inspected. Workmen dug at the foot of the grave until they reached the outer box, the end of which they opened. The detective peered inside and saw a coffin. Strangely, he did not open it and ordered that the hole be refilled.

In October, the widow Carrie caught wind of the detective's half-hearted inquiry and demanded that the sanctity of her husband's resting place be violated once more—and this time she wanted the coffin lid opened. When laborers pulled the outer box out of the ground, anyone could see it had been tampered with. The *Post* stated: "The head of the outer box had been broken off and in replacing it, so careless had been the person who unearthed the corpse that it had been placed back in a reverse position, the points of the nails sticking out." The responsible ghoul or ghouls had also stolen Elias's nameplate from the coffin as well as its nickel-plated handles. But the workmen opened the lid and there was Elias, right in his proper place.

Police located his lover Rose to ask if she knew who had vandalized Elias's piney abode. She confessed that she had been dating Eugene D., boss of the boneyard, who told her that in exchange for her exclusive attentions he would have Elias secretly exhumed and reburied in a private location so she could "weep barrels of tears" over him without the annoyance of facing Carrie. Eugene had fulfilled his sweet promise by the light of the midnight moon on July 26. The superintendent and two henchmen swiped the coffin's nameplate and handles "so that it could not be identified in case trouble came of it." The English language hasn't enough adjectives to describe such brilliance.

And so Rose had access to an exclusive grave for her former lover, at least until the story somehow got out. Then Eugene panicked and exhumed Elias's much-traveled corpse and reburied him in his original grave in case the cops came calling. Rose was angry over her new sweetheart's betrayal; hence, she sang like a canary to the detective. The superintendent and two conspirators were arrested for larceny.

Those who wish to go to Laurel Hill Cemetery and visit the grave of Elias and shed a few new tears on the well-watered spot will be disappointed. In 1892, 35,000 occupants of Laurel Hill were exhumed and moved to Cypress Lawn Cemetery in Daly City. In 1901, more bodies were reburied in the Japanese and Serbian cemeteries in Colma. The last remains in Laurel Hill were evicted in 1939. Elias's itinerant corpse kept traveling even after Rose was finished with him.

A Different Kind of Escort Service

Cast your mind about 130 years into the past. Your uncle Tuffy has climbed the Golden Stair, but his remains must be sent far away for burial—let's say Ho-Ho-Kus, New Jersey. Embalming is a widely accepted practice, so Tuffy can be preserved for a few days, at least, or until the chemicals wear off—whichever comes first. What is the best way to get him to Ho-Ho-Kus quickly? By express train! But how can you make certain that he will get there safely and on time? By hiring a "corpse escort," of course.

One such was Mary H., a middle-aged lady from Pasadena who made a career out of escorting bodies from Southern California to the East on behalf of the defunct's relatives. In 1889, a *Kansas City Times* reporter asked Mary about her peculiar career when she stopped in that city while on a return trip to California. "I have been in the business about two years," she said, "and I find that it is not uncongenial and pays better than anything else I can do."

She earned between $3 and $5 per day. The modern monetary equivalent of those sums is roughly $70 and $120 respectively, so Mary did pretty well for herself, especially considering that her arrangement included railroad fare and traveling expenses. Her best business came from relatives of invalids who had traveled to sunny California for their health and had died soon after.

Mary explained that hiring a corpse escort was downright economical: "Now, it costs double first-class express rates to send a body from California to the Missouri River, which amounts to about $300; consequently, it is cheaper to hire me, pay my expenses, and feel sure that the corpse will go through safely."

She concluded on an optimistic—for her—note: "The number of invalids who go to California is increasing every year, and my business is growing better."

Cemetery Strikers

The unionized gravediggers at Cypress Lawn Cemetery near San Francisco went on strike in June 1903. "Striking" meant that they vandalized their place of work. When the assistant superintendent and a workman—who were not union members—dug a grave, the strikers immediately filled it with water. The funeral had to wait until the hole was bailed out with buckets. Other graves received the same treatment.

The strikers also blew up a crematory by sprinkling crude oil on the furnace. They succeeded in thwarting a cremation, destroying part of the building, and seriously injuring two of their fellow workers—but that didn't matter since they weren't union men. Presumably the strikers did these things to draw sympathy to their cause.

The Original San Francisco Giants

Harold H., professor of zoology at Stanford, declared in December 1912 that the peninsula south of San Francisco was once home to a race of giants. He came to this conclusion after unearthing a prehistoric village covering nearly two acres, in which he found "several skeletons of men who were of unusual height." They did not appear to be brutes, however; the excavator found tools such as stone hammers, bone awls, and ornaments that "indicate[d] that their owners had attained considerable advancement in artisanship and civilization."

The Paths of Glory Lead but to the Grave

Abel Bennington C., a native of Kentucky, wanted the spiffiest tombstone his money could buy. In 1911, he purchased a plot in Los Angeles's Angelus Rosedale Cemetery for $135 and erected upon it a fifteen-foot granite monument with a marble base at a cost of $2,000. A stonemason chiseled Abel's name on it for $10.

It was one of the finest memorials in the graveyard, and Abel became obsessed with it. He would visit the monument monthly and polish it. Sometimes he read in its shadow.

Not content with his outer display of finery, Abel purchased a first-rate casket and a steel vault that was surely the envy of all his neighbors.

On March 8, 1922, Abel became ill at age eighty-eight. But by then he had spent his fortune on his tombstone and its accessories. He died a charity case in the county hospital on March 14 and was buried a pauper in a rich man's grave.

Swanky Sarcophagi

Sam K., a San Fernando Valley rancher, had a Los Angeles firm construct a special coffin for him in July 1925. It was a $1,200 steel number with a built-in radio. He explained that he wanted to keep up with the news until Judgment Day.

William B. was born in Stark County, Ohio, in 1834, came out West in the quest for gold in 1853, and ended his days in Shingle Springs, near Sacramento. He spent twenty years constructing his own cement-lined grave inside his corrugated iron shack on Bowman's Point, finally finishing construction in 1925 at age ninety-one. He even built a road stretching from the valley to the top of his hill for his mourners' greater convenience. He wished to be buried there instead of being carried to a tomb elsewhere.

William's idea was that when he sensed the Man in the Glowing Nightgown had come for him, he would climb into his coffin and pull a rope that would raise a semaphore signal. Then William's friends would know he was deceased.

An Early Cult Paves the Way

Young Willa R. died of natural causes in Los Angeles in 1926. She was the foster daughter of members of a cult called the Divine Order of the Royal Arm of the Great Eleven, a grandiose name even by cultish standards. Some people called the group by the less jaw-breaking name the Blackburn Cult.

Among the order's many peculiar tenets, they handled their own dead and operated secret cemeteries. Willa's body was kept on ice for nearly three years until her foster parents buried her under the floorboards of their house in early 1929—preserved in spices and salt and flanked by seven dead dogs—which was certainly much better.

By October 1929, the authorities were investigating the Divine Order because three members were missing and three others had passed away under fishy circumstances. One of these, Frances May T., had allegedly been baked alive in intervals in a brick oven over a two-day period as a cure for paralysis until Dr. Death ended the "treatment"; the death certificate of another, Harlene S., was not signed until several days after she'd passed unto her ancestors. Frances was buried secretly in San Gabriel and Harlene in Ventura.

The cult faced other, more earthly charges. A former member, wealthy oil operator Clifford D., filed charges of grand theft against the high priestess, May Otis B. He accused May of swindling him out of $40,000, which he had loaned her to finance a book she was writing along with her coauthors, the archangels Michael and Gabriel. The planned masterwork was to be titled *The Great Sixth Seal*, and it would reveal the hidden locations of precious minerals. As an incidental note, the book would also raise the dead, which was the reason Willa R. had initially been frozen rather than planted.

May countered that Clifford had voluntarily handed over the forty grand without expectation of recompense because the cult intended to elect him as the second messiah. It was an unusually weird he said, she said conundrum.

The cult leader went on trial in February 1930. On March 2, the jury found her guilty on eight counts, each of which carried a penalty of between one and fourteen years in prison. That marked the end of one of California's strangest cults (and that's saying a lot).

2
EIGHT MILLION PECULIAR WAYS TO DIE

A Boisterous Bozo

THE OFFICIAL DEATH RECORD FOR WILLIAM S., WHO DIED at age thirteen on January 11, 1854: "Killed by being swung around by the heels by a circus clown. Buried in Yerba Buena Cemetery, San Francisco, Cal., grave no. 3240."

According to the *Sacramento Daily Union*, "A post-mortem examination was held upon the body, the result of which proved to be that death was caused by a rupture of the left pulmonary artery. The Coroner's jury returned a verdict of death being produced by accident."

Perhaps circus clowns were more violent and in your face in those days. No matter what else happens to you today, at least you weren't swung by the heels by a clown.

Inventors and Inventive Deaths

Los Angeles amateur inventor Percy T., age thirty-three, was not prudent. Percy created an ointment that he thought would toughen human skin and make it bulletproof. This could give one army an advantage over another—and since World War I was going on at the time, he could sell his secret to the Allies. After smearing the ointment on himself every day for weeks, Percy chose August 28, 1915, as the day he would serve as his own guinea pig and, in his imagination, change world history. Using the last of his funds, he bought a revolver, a shotgun, and ammunition.

Percy applied the special lotion to his face and then shot himself three times in the countenance with the revolver. All three bullets penetrated his cheek. When he looked in the mirror he was badly disappointed.

The inventor's neighbors heard him shout, "Well, a bullet may be too heavy to stop just yet, but I know I can stop shot from a gun." So saying, he fired into his face with the shotgun and parted company with his lower jaw. Percy died the next day in the county hospital.

"The secret of his discovery died with him," said one press account, but frankly it doesn't sound like a secret worth knowing.

George M. of Long Beach was in a hurry to kill himself as he feared imminent arrest on a charge of assault with a deadly weapon. On February 16, 1929, he made his own electric chair by splitting the end of an unplugged lamp cord down the middle, then connecting each of the halves to two copper electrodes, which he held firm against his temples with a hat. Then it was a simple matter of sitting down and switching on the lamp. George left a note at his feet, which read, "God forgive me for what I am about to do."

Leroy I., a San Francisco mailman, fancied taking his own life with a homemade gas chamber and felt that he ought to take his wife, Charlotte, with him. On the night of April 4, 1937, he drugged her into insensibility and dropped poison pellets into a vase of acid. Death came on swift, silent wings for Leroy and Charlotte—and almost came for many other families in the three-story apartment building, who survived only due to Leroy's thoroughness. Before committing suicide, he had carefully taped over every crack and opening in the bedroom. Had he not taken this precaution, the many bodies of the unintentionally asphyxiated would have had to be stacked like cordwood.

Carl Y. of Los Angeles had the same great idea. He invented his own personal gas chamber on September 5, 1937, by setting up a Rube Goldberg-like device: when his alarm clock went off, its unwinding key lowered potassium cyanide tablets into a solution of sulfuric acid. The fumes filled Carl's trailer, and he met the Emperor of Ice Cream in short order. Like his inventive predecessor, Leroy I., Carl took care that his device should not take any unwilling victims; he taped a sign on the door reading "Danger! Poison. Only the law shall enter here." As a historical side note—just in case you are on a game show someday and the question comes up—he was the first person ever to commit suicide in a mobile home.

You Bet Your Life

One day in the winter of 1896, Henry R., a Texas rancher, sat in the lobby of New York's Fifth Avenue Hotel telling friends about a brutal card game he'd witnessed in Butte City, California, some thirty years before.

At the time of the incident, Henry had just completed a cattle drive among unsavory company: John W. ("who at that time bore the reputation of being the most daring cowboy in the West"), Fred D. ("a man with a record of four men"), Tobe H. ("a young desperado"), and Tom R. ("known all over the cattle countries as a murderous stock thief"). Adding to the volatility, John and Tom were enemies—apparently over some matter between Tom's deceased sister and John, but nobody knew the precise details.

After receiving their pay, the four took the stage to Butte and settled into the Old Cottage Hotel. Tom's sister happened to be buried in town, and he paid respects at her grave. When he returned, he joined the rest of the cowboys at Tip's Saloon to play high-stakes poker.

By three o'clock that morning, everyone had dropped out of the game except John and Tom. The latter had won most of the money; nevertheless, he was drunk and in an ugly frame of mind. At four o'clock, Tom—who had been drawing his pistol at the slightest provocation all evening—muttered, "If I lose this hand somebody is going to get killed."

As the sun rose, John bet $100. Tom bet $500, and John wagered another $500. Tom raised the stakes by another $500.

John pushed in a pile of his remaining money. "There is a thousand I'll go you better."

"Well," said Tom, "I'll see you that thousand and go you five hundred better."

"Haven't got it."

"Put up your horse and saddle, then."

John agreed, saying, "She goes."

"Now I've got you beat!"

"No, you haven't!" said John angrily.

Tom threw his gun on the table. "I'll bet you a thousand dollars against your life that I've got you beat."

John tried to smile. Rather than appear a coward, he agreed to the bet: "It goes."

(When recounting the story years later in the safety of the New York hotel lobby, Henry recalled that everyone at the table trembled and said not a word for two minutes.)

"I have called you," said John.

"I've got fours!"

"So have I."

"Not four aces!"

John trembled but said nothing.

"Not four kings," said Tom.

"Neither have you," replied John as he reached for a knife. "You haven't got four queens!"

"Neither have you," countered Tom.

John brightened. "Then I know pretty well you haven't got four jacks—there's my four tens!"

"Hold!" cried Tom. "Someone cheated."

"You lie!" John shouted.

Tom said, "Here's four jacks!" He threw the cards on the table and covered the pile of money with his hands.

In one deft movement, John drove his dagger through Tom's hands, fastening them to the table. Most of the onlookers cleared out of the saloon.

"I discarded one jack." John glowered.

But a check proved no one had cheated, and John realized with a sinking heart that he truly had lost the game—and much more besides. Sore loser John reached for his gun but found himself staring down the barrels of ten guns held by witnesses who were determined that he would abide by the wager.

The other cowboys pulled out the dagger that speared Tom's hands. As Tom collected his winnings, he said, "John, your life is mine, and I am going to have it."

"That's right," John joked lamely, "but it'll do me a lot of good and it won't do you any."

"You lost it to me and it's rightfully mine. You ought to know better than to use that knife of yours so devilishly freely, anyway."

Someone held John as Tom tied him. They marched him to the nearest hill and secured him to a tree.

"Are you ready, Tom?" called John.

"Yes," said the shaking, helpless man. "But I don't see why you want to take my life."

"It's mine."

Tom aimed two pistols at John's head and fired each twice. Then, feeling his drunkenness, he dropped a pistol and sank to the ground. "Blast it," he said. "He's paid the bet."

Suicide by Cacti

On the morning of January 17, 1892, travelers found the nude body of a man on the Cahuenga branch of the San Fernando Valley road, twelve miles from Los Angeles and south of Burbank. The ground was plowed up for hundreds of yards leading to the spot where the dead man lay exposed to the heat of day and the frost of night; whatever had happened to him, he must have fallen down repeatedly and thrashed around in the dirt before his substance turned to shadow. The puzzled travelers covered him with a piece of carpet and left him to the concern of the Los Angeles coroner.

That official observed several strange things about the death scene: the corpse was bruised and hideously, deeply lacerated; he appeared to have battered his head against the ground; his fingernails were torn and dirty. The only tracks were the dead man's, so he hadn't been murdered. And cactus thorns protruded from his body like quills on a defensive porcupine.

Four miles away, searchers found what appeared to be a freshly dug grave in hard clay soil. Opening it, they found the deceased's clothing, including his hat and shoes.

Putting these clues together, the coroner determined that the unknown man had dug a grave with his bare hands and buried his clothes in a fit of insanity, then ran naked through cactus patches until he died of his many, many injuries. The *San Francisco Chronicle*'s L.A. correspondent paid tribute to the single-minded determination that only madness can spawn: "He passed through places that would cause a man with thick clothing and heavy boots to shudder and turn back, and it is a wonder that he did not drop with exhaustion and loss of blood and pain long before he did."

Slow-Motion Suicide

In 1901, bookkeeper Ida Grace W. of Los Angeles was diagnosed as having tuberculosis. It was not a case of whether it would prove fatal, but when. So Ida bought a vial of strychnine while visiting Philadelphia, determined to end life on her own terms.

For the next three years, the disease wasted her body away; she carried the vial with her at all times, slowly working up her nerve. Yet she did not drink the poison until July 14, 1904. Afterward, she changed her mind and shouted for help, but it was too late. She was twenty-four.

For His Health

Burton J. of Terre Haute, a tubercular invalid, moved to California in 1906 for his health. On August 23, 1908, Burton visited an ostrich farm east of Los Angeles. Feeling faint, he stretched out under a tree—and couldn't get back up. Then swarm after swarm of red ants found him, and for two days Burton was eaten alive by the insects. Distant passersby saw him twitching and heard him crying out but assumed he was suffering from delirium tremens and did not come to his aid until it was too late. Burton died in the hospital on August 26.

J. J. D.'s Last Message

In October 1911, J. J. D., from Harrisonburg, Virginia, expired miserably twelve miles north of Bridgeport. He was working in the shaft of his gold mine when a falling rock pinned his left leg and he was unable to extricate himself. Though he was busy dying of hunger and exposure, J. J. D. wrote a daily diary on the back of an assay certificate:

> October 6—Frank, Yparraguirre, Sweetwater: If help does not come, send this message to M. C., wife, Harrisonburg, Va., and wire what to do with the body.—J. J. D.
> This occurred Friday afternoon, October 6. It is now Saturday, noon. No help yet. Why did this come?
> Sunday night—It is cold and long. God help me. I forgive mother.
> Monday—It is noon. Why did Dick forget? A drink of cold water would taste good. Am getting weak.
> Tuesday night—The end is near. Don't see how Dick can forget me.

Wednesday night—Guess tonight will be the last; no hope; the end is near.
Thursday—[Illegible.]
Friday, Noon—The thirteenth; no hope.

"Dick" was Richard B., a teamster at the Yparraguirre ranch and a friend of J. J. D's, who finally did find the unfortunate miner once—much too late—on October 28.

Oh, the Irony

Lee A. threw away the gift of life in Los Angeles on March 14, 1911, by drinking arsenic. He had once written a book called *How to Be Happy*.

Fred shot himself in the head in a mountain resort at Lake Arrowhead on December 17, 1928. As he entered the Void, he played on his phonograph "A Perfect Day," better known as "The End of a Perfect Day," a song written by his mother, Carrie. (Incidentally, the popular tune was also included in the songbooks on the *Titanic*.)

With a Proper Journalistic Closing

Harry, a Los Angeles newspaper reporter, freed his spirit by drinking poison at his desk on September 19, 1916. Coworkers found that he had written up a third-person news account about his own death. A few details were different: Harry had originally intended to shoot himself outside the office, but it appears he could not borrow a gun as originally planned. He wrote: "After writing the story of his death and suicide he had shot himself outside the newspaper office . . . The weapon he used to end his life was borrowed from [name deleted] on the pretext that Harry had been assigned on a story in a remote part of the city where frequent holdups have been committed." Harry ended the story in proper journalistic style with the notation "30."

Be Sure You're Right, Then Go Ahead

When William of Pomona took a trip to Los Angeles, he thought he saw his wife, Stella, fooling around with another man.

On July 8, 1922, twenty-three-year-old William swallowed mercury tablets in a funk of despair, but not before writing an extraordinary "will" in which he bequeathed Stella to "the other man": "I guess you thought I was only fooling, but now you know better. I am leaving you to the other man. If you can be happy with him, go to it and God bless you."

But had William done more sleuthing and less suiciding, he would have discovered that the woman he had seen in Los Angeles was actually his wife's twin sister, Selma.

Party Crasher

On October 3, 1923, John walked into a Los Angeles funeral home while a service was in progress. He walked up to the casket and belabored the obvious. "Is this a funeral?" he asked. When informed that it undeniably was, John stole the corpse's thunder by producing a pistol and shooting himself fatally in the head.

Happy Ending—Not!

Amandus cut his throat with a butcher knife and turned on the gas on August 5, 1929. The Oakland lawyer survived the suicide attempt and was amazed to find that the paralysis that had crippled his legs, fingers, and hands for years had mysteriously healed. "I never felt better in my life, and I want to live," announced Amandus. The doctors predicted he would recover, but Amandus passed away like a flower of the field ten days later.

She Did Not Leave Her Heart in San Francisco

A woman shot herself to death in a San Francisco hotel on June 10, 1933. She left a note requesting that she be cremated—that is, most of her. She wanted her heart to be sent to Dr. Ray S. of Western Reserve University in Cleveland.

Punctual Percy

A few minutes before five o'clock, on the evening of October 5, 1933, San Francisco broker Percy W. shot himself in his apartment. He left a note reading: "Report this at once. Sorry. But it is important from the standpoint of insurance that people know I died before 5 PM."

Had Percy pulled the trigger after five o'clock, his life insurance policy would have been null and void. Because he was punctual, his sister received $25,000.

Where Ignorance Is Bliss

San Francisco-born singer Russ Columbo's mode of death was bizarre—and what happened afterward was stranger yet.

In 1934, when the singing style known as crooning was in its heyday, twenty-six-year-old Russ was at the height of his popularity. Previously he'd had bit parts in several movies, but now he was debuting as the star of *Wake Up and Dream*, which highlighted his matinee idol good looks. He cowrote and performed a number of hit records, including "Time on My Hands" and "Just Another Romance"; "Prisoner of Love" (1931) remains his best-remembered song. His dance orchestra was one of the most admired in the nation. He was reportedly earning a salary of $7,500 a week (modern equivalent: more than $100,000 a week). And to top it all, the lucky guy was dating Carole Lombard!

On September 2, only three days after his starring movie was released, Russ visited his friend Lansing B., a Hollywood portrait photographer. Lansing owned a century-old French dueling pistol and wanted Russ to see it. The first mistake was that neither checked to see if it was loaded. Lansing absentmindedly squeezed the trigger repeatedly with no effect.

The second mistake occurred when Lansing, craving a cigarette, lit a match and held it too close to the gun.

Not only did the antique pistol have a lead ball in it, it also contained a potent charge of gunpowder. Lansing accidentally dropped the match on the cap. The pistol fired, sending the ball into a mahogany dresser. It ricocheted and entered Russ's brain through his left eye. He died at the hospital a few hours later without regaining consciousness. "It was quite obviously an accident, an act of God," said his brother, Jack, sadly.

Two days before the accident, the singer's mother, Julia, had had severe heart attack. When Russ died, she was still in critical condition in a Santa Monica hospital. Her friends and family decided not to tell her about her famous son's death out of fear that the shock would prove fatal.

And they *continued* not to tell her, even after the imminent danger of heart failure had passed. They entered a solemn pact to keep the news from Julia. That meant keeping her away from the radio and newspapers. On December 22, she received a cable wishing her a merry Christmas from a conspirator pretending to be Russ.

So began a long stream of weekly letters and cables, putatively from Russ, telling her about his world tours and adventures in Hollywood and what a swell time he was having and wishing he wasn't so busy so he could come home for a visit. Every now and then, the faux-Russes also sent spending money. Julia was nearly blind; thus the letters were read aloud to her. Had she been able to read the missives herself, she might have noticed that the handwriting wasn't her son's.

Russ's parents celebrated their fiftieth wedding anniversary on December 13, 1936. Julia found it a happy occasion "despite the inability of Russ to attend," reported a news article.

Every month she received a check for $398 from "Russ." It was actually money from a double-indemnity insurance policy the singer had taken out in 1932.

As late as September 1939, Julia still hadn't realized that the letters were fraudulent. Calling it a "humane deception," a newspaper remarked, "Perhaps now she could stand the shock. But why tell her the sad news after all these years?" Her physician added: "She is happy in the belief that her son is a great success."

Carole Lombard helped keep up the ruse until her own tragic death in a plane crash in 1942.

Julia died on August 30, 1944—an entire decade after her son—unaware to the end of his strange and untimely accident. The efforts to keep the knowledge from her were widely reported in the press at the time, so it's something of a miracle that she never found out.

Why Not Make a Game of It?

On February 1, 1935, W. H. B. of Los Angeles found a suicide note from his brother, Otto, written in the form of a treasure hunt. It told W. H. to go to the 4300 block of Fountain Street "for further directions."

W. H. B. went there and found another note instructing him to go to the 800 block of North Brand Boulevard.

At that location, another note said to go to the 2000 block of Hillhurst.

On that street was a fourth note telling him to go to the end of Alta Vista Street in Glendale. W. H. B. followed the instructions, and in Glendale he found Otto's body sitting in a car, asphyxiated with carbon monoxide fumes.

Getting Nailed

Dema D. of Pinole, age twenty-two, schemed up a unique way to end her life: she pounded a four-inch steel spike into her skull over her left ear on the night of February 22, 1937, and then went to bed awaiting the appearance of the Death Angel. But he was tardy, and in the morning, Dema "hesitantly" (in the words of the press) told her mother, Gladys, what she had done—as though there was any way she could hide it. Gladys rushed her to the hospital at Berkeley, where medical experts did all they could. Dema's tomorrows stopped coming on February 25.

Exit Laffin'

Seaman Cecil Roy J. was stationed on the USS *Barry* in San Diego. On June 3, 1937, he tied an anchor to his leg and leaped overboard. He had just enough time to shout "Some fun, eh, kid?" at a fellow sailor before he entered the billowy waves.

Home Body

Alice J. of Los Angeles had a strange mania for hiding from people. She went to a rest home from which she disappeared on December 14, 1936.

The mystery was solved on June 20, 1937, when ten-year-old Malcolm crawled under the house to retrieve a stray baseball. He found the partly mummified—but far from pristine—remains of Alice who had, police theorized, wriggled under the building to hide and died of exposure.

Sartorial Splendor Gone to Waste

On November 18, 1937, Dock D. of Bakersfield put on his very spiffiest suit and then placed eight lit sticks of dynamite under his head, which would seem to defeat the purpose of the suit.

Poisoned Paupers

William D. and his wife, Olive, poisoned and shot themselves on the stone steps of a Glendale schoolhouse on June 13, 1938. The motive for their suicide pact was that their $9 million fortune had dwindled to one dollar.

Temporary Reprieve

Averill C. of Oakland concluded that life was a burden. On the night of July 10, 1938, he turned on the gas in his bedroom and stretched out to take that final sleep. He awoke the next morning feeling relieved that his plan had failed. Then he lit a victory cigarette, and—

Averill survived long enough to tell the police what had happened.

Macho Mistake

Robert Louis G., a guard at Folsom Prison, had a most idiotic hobby: he enjoyed showing envious prisoners how much electricity he could take by holding a fifty-five-volt line and a ground wire. Robert found out his limit on May 19, 1939, when he accidentally stepped in a puddle while demonstrating his superpowers before a crowd of convicts.

3

STRANGE CIRCUMSTANCES

Don't Say You Weren't Warned

IN 1882, DR. E. T. W., RESIDENT PHYSICIAN AT THE STATE Asylum at Napa, crunched the numbers and declared that it wouldn't be long until much of the state of California was insane: "If the ratio of increase continues as it has done in the past twenty years, one-third of the population of the state will be insane by the end of the century."

But by 1888—a mere six years later!—the situation looked even worse. The Napa asylum was constructed in 1876 for 600 patients; only twelve years later, it held 1,450 with no sign of abatement. Lunatics were housed two to a cell; some even slept in the hallways. The asylum at Stockton was so overcrowded that the state announced plans to build a third one.

The doctor observed that most of California's insane were immigrants from Germany or Ireland, that 33 percent of the state's insanity was "directly or indirectly caused by alcoholic drinks," and that San Francisco furnished the most madmen. But the bleakest news of all, the doctor told his friend E. A. M.

of the St. Louis Women's Christian Temperance Union, was that "if the ratio continues to increase in the future as it has in the past, a little calculation may show the time when the whole state will be mad and neighboring states will be called on to care for California's insane."

All of this, of course, neatly explains the Los Angeles Freeway.

California's Pygmalion

Wealthy William B. seemed a normal enough fellow—in 1907, he was the superintendent of the electrical plant at Fort Bragg—but he had one outstanding eccentricity in which he luxuriated. Disappointed in love in his youth, he wanted a family but did not wish to experience the potential heartbreaks. His ingenious solution was to carve a life-sized spouse and six children out of wood.

William and his piney family lived in an eight-room house. The "wife" and "children" wore the best clothes William could purchase; a dressmaker provided the bejeweled missus with the latest fashions. Neighbor ladies left calling cards at the residence.

The man of the house enjoyed holding receptions for his daughters and posing his wife and kids in various scenes of domestic bliss: reading novels, sitting at the dinner table, making beds, working at the sewing machine. He also bought presents for his faux family.

When his oldest daughter, Jane, wanted to get married, William carved a suitable husband for her (lest she break his heart, one presumes, by marrying a lowlife mannequin from a dime store).

A correspondent for the *Chicago Tribune* waxed whimsical when describing William's family:

> There are many advantages in having such a family as this one, for the wife can never quarrel with her husband, no matter how late he may return from the lodge. The daughters can never elope, for their father has only to chop them up into kindling wood if they become refractory in such matters and as for the

sons, if they refuse to follow their father's footsteps he has only to put them into the stove and they will help make the house comfortable.

The magazine section of the *San Francisco Call* of October 21, 1906, featured photos of the family.

Doings of the Deranged

Mary H. of Berkeley thought the spirits of two deceased cousins were out to get her. The smart way to handle this, she decided, was to baffle them by ascending in a cloud of smoke. She stuffed the kitchen stove full of paper, lit it, and made herself comfortable on the range. That's where her husband found her "sitting calmly" when he came home from work. On October 10, 1904, Mary was arrested on a charge of insanity.

Alta F., age twenty, fancied herself a natural-born killer. "I had terrible impulses to kill or harm even my best friends," she explained. She thought her murderous urges entered her brain through her right arm, so to keep from becoming a killer, she did the only sensible thing: on September 6, 1930, she stuck her arm under a moving train at Pacific Grove. Alta survived the amputation, suffering nothing worse than shock. As far as the record shows, she never murdered anyone.

Professor Roger S. taught at the University of California at Berkeley for eight years. On August 4, 1919, after his job was terminated, Roger strolled to Gilman Hall and shot Professor Edmond O., head of the chemistry department, and assistant professor J. H. H. Both survived, but Roger was no longer welcome in academia.

The original Nutty Professor spent the next thirteen years at the state asylum at Napa. Doctors thought his mental condition was improving, and eventually he was considered so harmless they granted him permission to stroll about the grounds unmonitored.

On January 9, 1932, the ex-professor made asses of his doctors by placing his head on the tracks of the Napa Electric Railway and thereby cleanly decapitating himself before dozens of interested onlookers.

As for Gilman Hall, plutonium was identified as an element there in 1941.

On the night of July 12, 1934, eight-year-old Elaine W. of Ingleside wandered into the yard of her neighbor, unemployed mechanic Albert R., to look for her pet white rabbit. Albert beat the child to death with a whisky bottle and half-buried her in his basement. He also killed her rabbit and put it in a stew.

Albert denied the crime at first but confessed when the Ingleside police made him look at Elaine's body. He could hardly have expected his protestations of innocence to be taken seriously, because Elaine's playmate Irene had seen Albert invite Elaine into his basement. Not only that, his wife's fourteen-year-old niece, Elsie, said that when Uncle Albert had come up from the basement he'd told her, "I've just killed a girl, and if you don't believe it, I'll bring the body upstairs and throw it in your face."

Albert went on trial two months later. At first he pled not guilty due to insanity, but at the last minute changed his plea to guilty. On September 17, he was sentenced to life at San Quentin.

After a few years in prison, Albert claimed that he had spent a whole day plotting Elaine's murder. He said he wanted to commit suicide and thought going to the gas chamber would be a good way to do it. So, said Albert, what appeared to be a hopelessly bungled murder-on-impulse was actually "the perfect murder"— he had wanted to get caught and pay the supreme penalty all along! The governor was unimpressed, and on November 13, 1939, he upheld the original sentence.

There was talk in some circles that Albert might be insane after all.

Raymond H. ran to a San Francisco traffic cop on August 25, 1938, and said by way of a greeting: "I've just killed my wife." To prove his point, Raymond produced a piece of human flesh from his pocket.

At Raymond's address, police found Jean H. strangled on the bed and mutilated with a hunting knife. Her husband had written "Honey I love you" on her abdomen and left a maudlin love letter on the dresser, addressed "To sweetheart from darling."

For a grand finale, Raymond hanged himself in his jail cell on January 2, 1939, as he awaited trial. He left a note stating that he hoped he would be buried beside Jean.

Richard J. of Los Angeles was only fourteen but big and strong for his age. His record for juvenile delinquency began when he was six; he was sentenced to the reformatory at Whittier at age thirteen for a series of petty thefts and was released in June 1939. His criminal career ended on a spectacular note on August 22 when his playmate of only two days, thirteen-year-old Billy W., teased him for being "an ex-convict" as the boys played in a dug-out section under Richard's residence.

A few minutes later, Richard's mother, Frances, heard a noise "like a dog growling." She poked her head out the window. "Richard, what's that noise?" she asked.

"Billy's dog swallowed a tack," said Richard.

Next, Frances heard a sound she described as "a yowling as though the boys were torturing a cat." This time she was disturbed enough to go outside and investigate. "What's going on under there, Richard?"

"Don't come under here, Ma. I've just killed Billy."

Frances ran next door and told Billy's mother, Ellen, who inched into the crawlspace. Richard had crushed Billy's head with a hammer, strangled him with a wire, and stabbed him three times near the heart with a butcher knife and sheep shears. He was still alive but died soon afterward.

Showing precocity far beyond his years, Richard told police psychiatrists that he'd intended to cut up Billy's body and bury the pieces. He'd gotten the idea from a detective magazine he'd read in the very reformatory that intended to turn him into a model citizen.

At the coroner's inquest, Superior Judge Ben L. referred to Richard as "the most callous and cold-blooded individual I have seen in thirty-five years of courtroom experience."

On September 18, Richard was declared not of sound mind and sentenced to be confined at the State Hospital for the Insane, thereby sparing society from God knows what in the future.

Bill Doesn't Know His Own Strength

Bill W. died at age eighty-one in the last week of October 1933. In life, he was noted in San Francisco for two things. One was the great pride he placed in his muscular physique. The other was an accident that he'd caused—or rather, that he *thought* he'd caused.

Early on the morning of April 18, 1906, Bill entered a saloon at Fourth and Townsend thirsting for a gin fizz. He had no money but thought he could get a drink on credit.

"No drink, no credit," said the bartender.

Bill's pride in his strength came to the fore. "White man," said he, "you all better fix up that gin fizz or I'm gonna pull down this here bar."

The bartender sneered.

Bill grabbed the bar and shook it as hard as he could. At that moment, the San Francisco earthquake took down the saloon as well as more than 80 percent of the city.

For the rest of his life, Bill was convinced he was the one-man cause of the quake. "It was the water pipes," he would say. "They was all fastened together all over town. When I give that there jerk I musta pulled on the faucet in the saloon and brung down the whole works."

The Original Hunger Game

J. A. M., a resident of Foresthill in Placer County, was notorious in the 1880s for his appetite, which covered the range from merely excessive to disgusting. On one memorable occasion, he consumed eight cans of oysters, several cans of peaches, and a quantity of crackers, cheese, and bologna, not to mention an estimated eight to ten glasses of beer. When someone asked him to entertain his obviously highbrow audience with a song afterward, J. A. M. demanded to know if they expected him to sing on an empty stomach.

J. A. M. was also known to eat flies by the handful, and once he consumed a mouse to win a bet of $1.50. But the glutton's "galvanized, elastic stomach" proved a drawback in the summer of 1884, when he ineffectually attempted suicide by swallowing strychnine.

Stanford's Stash

Industrialist Leland Stanford financed the founding of the California university that bears his name. However, his brother, Thomas Welton Stanford (some sources give his middle name as Wellington) gave the university a donation that was less welcome.

T. W. Stanford was deeply interested in the occult and spent much of his time and money traveling to exotic places and collecting such arcana as idols, fetishes, books on spiritualism, and apports (physical objects that are allegedly produced by the spirit world).

After living in Australia for many years, T. W. Stanford had accumulated boxes and boxes' worth of these mystical artifacts. On August 28, 1918, he died in Melbourne. Twenty years before his death, rumor had held that he intended to donate

$15 million to the university; this was untrue, but he did give a number of books, manuscripts, and pictures about Australia. Also, he bequeathed his vast collection of supernatural tomes and trinkets to the university.

This put the trustees in a ticklish position. They couldn't politely turn down a bequest from the founder's brother, nor did they wish to put the collection on public display. They compromised by consigning the entire stash to a locked room where none of it would see the light of day. With time, the collection was, by and large, forgotten.

Novelist Idwal Jones heard about the donation and requested permission to see it. Authors Brad Williams and Choral Pepper described his quest in their 1967 book *The Mysterious West*:

> He had considerable difficulty in locating anyone who knew of the incident and its temporary solution, but eventually he located a Professor Coover of the Department of Psychology who was aware of it. The professor spent several hours searching for a key, then accompanied Jones to the "Occult Room" hidden away on a colonnade. The collection was still there, untouched, covered with dust. Writing on a small box, barely legible, labeled its contents as "prepared rat entrails." A small sheaf of sea grass lay withered on the floor. Crates of books were piled from floor to ceiling and in one corner was an assortment of weapons ranging from spears to tiny daggers.

Williams and Pepper asked if they, too, could see the collection. They mentioned the trouble Idwal Jones and Professor Coover had finding the room's key. "Oh no, it's a little more than that," a Stanford official said. "They know it's around somewhere, but this time they appear to have lost the room."

There is—or recently was, anyway—a Thomas Welton Stanford Chair for Psychical Research at Stanford University. There is also a T. W. Stanford Art Gallery.

Noggin Nugget

"More gold has been mined from the mind of men than the earth itself."—Napoleon Hill

In October 1939, a miner at Rattlesnake Bar unearthed a human skull. He didn't want to keep the perpetually grinning reminder of his own mortality, so he gave it to a Chinese miner. He, in turn, washed the cranium in a creek and found a ten-ounce gold nugget rattling around where the brain was once housed. Moral: If someone gives you the gift of a skull, don't turn it down.

4
OTHERWORLDLY WISE: COASTAL GHOSTS

Farfetched Frisco Phantoms

AN OLD TWO-STORY FRAME HOUSE THAT STOOD FOR YEARS on the corner of Larkin Street and Willow Avenue in San Francisco acquired such a reputation for ghostliness that no one would rent it. In December 1884, the house's owner moved it to Twenty-Seventh and Castro Streets, but potential tenants still refused to take the bait. If anything, the new location seemed to make the ghosts even more industrious. According to the *San Francisco Chronicle*, "the neighborhood has been kept in a constant dread and torment by unearthly groans, mysterious lights, and agonized shrieks emanating from this dread habitation."

On December 22, three neighborhood residents—R. D. G., William C., and George K.—joined forces to investigate the house, convinced that the phenomena were the work of practical jokers. As they approached the house, a tall, white-robed spirit strode toward them out of the gloom. The men took especial notice of its "awful, calm, and majestic mien" and the utter silence of its advance. Panic-stricken, R. D. attempted to slash at it with a knife, but his friends stopped him. When the ghost got within ten feet of them, it vanished in a downward motion as though descending a flight of stairs. (The next day, R. D. examined the place where the figure disappeared and found no steps.) The would-be paranormal researchers raced down the sidewalk in panic. Half a block from the haunted house they encountered a second ghost, which vanished as they approached.

After gathering their wits and nerve, R. D. and George chose to have another go at the house that night. (William, it appears, decided he had other things to do.) On their second foray, they brought three other men.

When they ventured near the house at midnight, the building seemed enveloped in blue light as sobs and cries echoed from within, which they took to be the lamentations of a number of spirits, showing ghosts' usual disregard for live people who must sleep and go to work in the morning. After that, the men heard someone singing a loud dirge. A pair of specters became visible for a few seconds. As soon as these vanished, a third figure appeared just beyond the house on the hillside overlooking the Noe Valley. The unnerved men followed and threw many rocks at it at short range, but it disappeared unharmed, leaving in its wake a pair of dogs that seemed dazzled by the unearthly light it produced.

The investigators felt at this juncture that they should go home.

The Second Subject

The history of "spirit photography" is rife with hoaxes, frauds, and honest mistakes, but an incident from Los Angeles in 1890 features points of interest. The correspondent who originally sent the story to the *St. Louis Globe-Democrat* insisted the story was true.

A woman having her portrait taken in a leading gallery struck a winsome pose; the photographer placed his head under the cloth attached to the camera, as required by the technology of the time. He emitted a startled shout. Then his head came out from under the cover. Plainly frightened, he asked the subject, "Did anyone pass behind you just then?"

"Certainly not," replied the lady.

The photographer went to the darkroom to develop the photo. He came out a few minutes later, ashen-faced. "You'll have to sit again," he said.

The same scene was reenacted. She posed; he put his head under the cover and took the picture then emerged with a terrified expression, a perspiring face, and shaking hands. Again the photographer went to the darkroom and came back a few minutes later palpably afraid. The woman had to have her picture taken five times in all. The photographer explained neither his mounting terror nor his reason for the numerous retakes.

Finally, he told his annoyed customer that they would have to go to another location; he could not take her picture there. She demanded an explanation. After a considerable delay—and likely with an air of "you'll wish you hadn't asked"—he showed her the five developed photos. Each showed a second figure standing beside the woman: a recently deceased acquaintance dressed in grave clothes and with an arm outstretched.

The woman nearly fainted but declared the whole business a hoax until the photographer convinced her that he was as surprised as she. The woman was so alarmed that she soon became seriously ill.

So what happened next? Unfortunately, there is no way to tell since the report named neither of the persons involved. Both the woman and the photographer were described as disbelievers in ghosts and skeptical about Spiritualism.

Scaring Up Some Justice

Zelia G. was found dying in Los Angeles on October 30, 1913. She—or someone—had placed a sealed hatbox snugly around her neck; a small hole in the box accommodated a tube leading to a gas jet. Zelia died shortly after she was found. Detectives suspected her druggist husband, John, of poisoning her and then rigging up said contraption to make it look like suicide by asphyxiation. He, on the other hand, claimed she was a genuine suicide. A coroner's jury agreed with John, but police exhumed her anyway. Pathologists found poison in her vital organs.

When police arrested John on the night of January 24, 1914, they thought applying third-degree tactics might get a confession. Therefore, they took John to a dark room in the apartment where his wife had died. Suddenly a ghost appeared and bawled, "Whyyyyy did you muuuuurder meeeee?" The druggist wasn't impressed by the spectral visitation and did not confess. With good cause: Zelia's revenant was only too obviously a woman in a white robe smeared with phosphorescent varnish.

Police Judge Joseph wasn't impressed either, and on February 6, he dismissed charges on the grounds that the state had not established a case. But on May 13, John was arrested in Waterville, Maine, for having attempted to murder Zelia by asphyxiation in a Portland hotel six months before she died in L.A. Let's hope the Waterville police had a good enough case against John that they didn't send out someone wrapped in a glow-in-the-dark bedsheet.

The Ghost of Honor

The following social item appeared in the papers in March 1922: "A dinner was held in Los Angeles March 23, given by the Longer Life League in honor of Dr. James Martin Peebles." The attendees declared that Dr. Peebles personally attended the feast. Remarkable if true, since the guest of honor—a noted Spiritualist as well as an author and physician—had shaken hands with the Reaper on February 15.

An empty chair stood at the speakers' table. The toastmaster said to the three hundred attendees: "He is with us, sitting in this chair. Some of you who are clairvoyants may be able to see him." The late Dr. Peebles told everyone—using the toastmaster as his mouthpiece—that he was no longer plagued with rheumatism and had been having a gala time exploring the moon.

Among Dr. Peebles's notable achievements, other than postmortem lunar exploration, was a popular book entitled *How to Live a Century and Grow Old Gracefully* (1884). He fell only a few weeks short of his goal, having been born on March 23, 1822. Also, judging from his photos, he had one heck of a beard.

5

PREDATORS AND PREY: TRUE CRIME STORIES

A Hairbreadth from Death

RUSSIAN POLE JAN (OR JON) WASIELEWSKY MURDERED HIS former wife at Los Gatos on June 9, 1882. He was sentenced to be hanged at San Jose on October 23, 1884. That city's correspondent to the *Daily Alta California* wrote in anticipation: "The cur-like nature of the murderer, and his cowardly disposition, promise to make the execution afford a feast for those who revel in the horrible, and Jan's taking off is expected to be unexcelled in sickening details." By "cowardly disposition" the author meant that the condemned man had spent his final hours pretending to be insane and fooling absolutely no one. He had also made an attempt to starve himself but gave up and afterward ate up to six meals a day.

One feature in particular made Jan's execution an event well worth walking many a weary mile to see: he was literally hanged by a hair. The gallows was constructed with a series of counterweights so well balanced that a single human hair held all the mechanisms in place. When the murderer was benoosed and placed on the trapdoor, the hangman cut the hair, causing a fourteen-pound weight to fall and spring the trap.

Despite the prediction by the *Daily Alta California* that the hanging would be a cornucopia of "sickening details," the whole affair went off perfectly. In a final poetic touch, the hair used to stretch Jan's neck came from the head of his victim.

Hangings, Legal and Otherwise

Joe "Hooch" S. shot banker Jim A. at Skidoo on April 19, 1908. When the *Los Angeles Herald* got wind of the murder, the editor sent a reporter to get the scoop. Sadly for the reporter, and incidentally also for Hooch, by the time the newshound got to Skidoo the citizens had already lynched Hooch from a telegraph pole and buried him on April 22. Residents felt sorry for the disappointed reporter, so for his benefit they exhumed Hooch and hanged him again so the journalist could return home with a story and a picture.

Ed Williams, an Indian, was sent to San Quentin's Death Row for getting drunk and killing Inez B., with whom he lived. He got several reprieves but announced in November 1912 that he didn't want any more; if he was destined to be hanged, he wanted it done soon. Before he was suspended on November 29, 1912, Ed requested that the prison band put on a concert for him. They played for three hours, though it was noted that "some of them [were] perspiring with nervousness."

An African American named Thomas G. was lynched in Joplin, Missouri, on April 14, 1903. The result was a race riot in which a row of Negro cabins was burned. One woman was killed, and her son Edward Delehantie swore that he would take revenge—not on the people who'd actually murdered his mother, which would have been somewhat sensible, but on white folks in general.

Edward was eventually sentenced to fourteen years for criminal assault and ended up in Folsom State Prison in Sacramento, where he killed a fellow inmate. He was hanged on December 6, 1912. Before the execution, musicians serenaded him; Edward played a recording of William Jennings Bryan's speech, "Immortality"; and the condemned man anticipated Monty Python by many decades by recording himself singing "Always Keep on the Sunny Side."

Willard "Red" Shannon murdered Stockton car salesman Harold L. on December 31, 1926. On May 4, 1928, the night before his execution, Red amused himself by listening to "The Sidewalks of New York" repeatedly on a phonograph and by reading the latest issue of the *Saturday Evening Post*. The magazine was running the final installment of Earl Derr Biggers's Charlie Chan mystery "Behind That Curtain," and Red wanted to see how it ended.

On November 2, 1930, twenty-two-year-old mother Merle E. was shotgunned as she lay beside her infant son. In such a case the spouse is generally the prime suspect, and the Los Angeles police took the victim's estranged husband, Emory E., in for questioning. During interrogation, Mr. E. casually mentioned someone named Benjamin Franklin B.

Benjamin, an itinerant glassblower described as a "slight, gentle-looking man," was also brought in on November 5. His conscience troubled him, and he confessed that Emory had hired him to murder the woman. The pathetic amateur hitman had been promised $2,000 to do the job, but Emory could give him a down payment of only $2.00—all in dimes. (Some accounts state that Benjamin was given $2.20; if true, he must have really lived it up on that extra twenty cents.)

On January 16, 1931, Benjamin was sentenced to hang while Emory received a life sentence. Benjamin paid the ultimate debt to society on July 31.

Dallas E. shot William K. during a holdup in Los Angeles in July 1933. A half hour before he was hanged at San Quentin on October 21, Dallas drank whisky and marched to the gallows to a sprightly jazz tune. He went to his Maker calmly, but three shaken witnesses had to be assisted out of the death chamber.

Their Song Was "Clair de Lune"

"Each man kills the thing he loves."—Oscar Wilde, *The Ballad of Reading Gaol*

If it is true that life imitates art, then the story of that unlikeliest of murderers, Leslie Gireth, is like a *film noir* come true. Yet until the events were set in motion that led to his downfall, Leslie's life was a shining example of what could be accomplished with determination and hard work.

Leslie was born on August 25, 1903, in Hungary. He immigrated to the United States in 1926 after studying law at the University of Budapest. Those who knew Leslie were not stingy with praise; he was a cultured, courteous man who radiated Old World charm. Newspaper photos reveal that he was matinee-idol handsome. He made his way to Redondo, California, where he worked at Imre's jewelry store. He fell in love with the boss's daughter, Mary Anna, five years his junior. Imre gave the couple his blessing and his thriving business. Leslie and Mary were married on August 29, 1929. Eventually the couple moved to Glendale and started a second jewelry store and bought a house. Within a few years, they were the parents of two sons. Despite the Great Depression, Leslie prospered and became the director of the Glendale Chamber of Commerce and Rotary Club.

Although Leslie's life may have seemed perfect to onlookers, cracks were secretly forming. The legal record paints a portrait of a troubled marriage. Leslie complained that his wife drank heavily, ignored his physical needs, deliberately served inedible meals, and antagonized him by hiding his soap, toothpaste, and shaving accessories. Then there was the time she allegedly attacked him with a butcher knife. Mary countered with charges of adultery and complained that he was "not conventional in his desires" (something he vehemently denied). She also claimed that he was trying to seize complete control of their jewelry store. The enmity between them was so great by 1940 that Mary attempted to have her husband prosecuted for violating an immigration law. The couple separated in February 1942.

Perhaps eventually Leslie and Mary would have worked things out or gotten divorced. But the catalyst that made tragedy inevitable entered Leslie's life in summer 1941. She was Dorena, a student at San Jose State College who was taking classes in meteorology at Boeing School of Aeronautics with a view to working for an airline. Friends described her as "vivacious," and she reportedly had "lots of boyfriends." She took a part-time job at the jewelry store, and soon the proprietor and his employee were in love, although Leslie was married and nearly twice her age. They managed to keep the affair private, but Dorena's parents found out and were not shy about voicing their disapproval. Mary did not know about the courtship until later, though Leslie had already spent some time in the marital doghouse for romancing a different salesgirl.

Leslie and Dorena enjoyed romantic interludes on weekends. Photos show them embracing and kissing. Leslie later remarked sadly, "Sometimes you meet a person like that.... You do the little things, the crazy beautiful things, and the world and life are wonderful... just because you are together." These little things included dining on their favorite snack, hamburgers and Cokes, while listening to classical music. One piece in particular was so beloved by them that they considered it "their song": Debussy's "Clair de Lune."

The happy times lasted precisely one year. Thursday, July 16, 1942, commemorated the anniversary of their first date. On that day, Leslie and Dorena were staying at the luxurious Casa del Monterey motor court in San Leandro. (They checked into cabin number ten as "Leslie and wife.") They ate hamburgers and drank Cokes. After Dorena went to sleep, Leslie shot her twice in the temple and once in the chest at point-blank range with a .25-caliber automatic pistol. He spent the next several hours contemplating his deed and obsessively playing "Clair de Lune" on a phonograph. Finally, he left the scene, telling the auto court owner that his "wife" was sick in bed and should not be disturbed. Leslie then fled to Fresno, two hundred miles away. The next day he decided to turn himself in. He called the Oakland police and told them what he had done, where the body was located, and where he could be picked up. Fresno officers arrested Leslie in a hotel lobby.

A bizarre tableau awaited the police when they opened the San Leandro cabin. Dorena lay neatly tucked in bed, two days dead and clad only in a green silk pajama top, as the phonograph played "Clair de Lune" repeatedly. Leslie had placed a brightly colored ribbon in her hair. A table beside the bed bore a framed photo of Leslie, arranged in such a way that Dorena's dead eyes stared upward at it. On the back of the picture was written: "Dorena, my darling—humble words could never express how I love you, how I adore you. Always remember that. Your Les." Near the photo was a vase full of red carnations. (The members of the press felt remiss in their duties in those days if they failed to give each new killer a headline-grabbing nickname, so in honor of this discovery Leslie was dubbed the Red Carnation Killer.) The couple's love letters were at the scene, and both the *L.A. Times* and the *San Francisco Chronicle* quoted choice passages. Also at the site was a bottle of expensive perfume Leslie had purchased for Dorena the day he murdered her. Its name was I Will Return.

Leslie refused to talk about his motives, other than to imply that he could not bear to be without his girlfriend, yet he realized that their relationship was bad for her: "I was afraid that our interest in each other might lead to scandal that would ruin her life. It's a long story and people wouldn't understand."

He claimed that he could not remember shooting her: "It was all as though it were fate." He granted a remarkable interview to a sympathetic *San Francisco Chronicle* reporter, who noted that for Leslie "nothing is real anymore. This is a dream, or it is death in life." The prisoner said, "It is a strange thing. A million things are going through your mind. And suddenly it is done, and you don't know why you did it. . . . There was no trouble. We never had an argument in the year we knew each other. . . . She went to sleep. I lay there in the dark, thinking the millions of things." But he did not tell the reporter, the police, or the psychiatrist who examined him before the trial anything specific about the "millions of things" that went through his mind and persuaded him to reach for his gun.

Leslie was arraigned in San Leandro on July 20. The defense attorney urged him to plead temporary insanity, but his client had other ideas. "I feel as though I have lost the most precious thing in the world," he told the San Francisco reporter. "I do not care much what happens to me. I am ready to pay any price." When he appeared in court he seemed calm, apathetic, and listless. He pled guilty, adding that he was ready to "take his medicine." He was indicted by an Oakland grand jury on July 24 and arraigned soon afterward. His attorney told the press that Leslie said, "It would be better for my children if I were out of the way entirely. I want to die and get it over with."

It is an evil habit to waste sentiment upon deliberate murderers, yet it is difficult not to feel sympathy for Leslie, who killed the thing he loved. When he faced Superior Judge Lincoln Church on August 4, Leslie refused legal representation and withdrew his request for a jury trial. The judge was so surprised that he temporarily called a halt to the proceedings. Six days later, Judge Church found Leslie guilty and sentenced him to die in the gas chamber at San Quentin. Leslie was so determined to rejoin Dorena that he more or less forced the judge to reach that grimmest of verdicts. He pled guilty, manfully declined to take the "temporary insanity" cop-out, would not accept legal aid, and would not take the stand in his own defense. He refused even to give a motive for murdering Dorena, which might have played well with a sympathetic judge. Dorena's father told the press: "I am satisfied. My girl was vivacious and unsophisticated. For the horror and shame he brought on us, I hope the man that killed her suffers the tortures of hell."

Because Leslie did not explain his actions, the public speculated wildly. Three theories seem plausible. The first was implied by Leslie himself when he told the police shortly after his arrest: "I was afraid that our interest in each other might lead to scandal that would ruin her life." Leslie's attorney described Mary as "vindictive." Perhaps Leslie, fearing that his estranged wife would go public when she found out about the affair, decided on a mercy killing to spare Dorena the humiliation. He may also have kept his silence out of consideration for the two families involved. A few days before his execution, he still refused to reveal his motive to reporters: "At this stage of things, it isn't [about] myself anymore. If you print things against me you are doing it not to me, but to my two children, whom I love, to the girl's family, whom I respect and love, and other people."

The second theory was more cynical: some held that Leslie murdered his girlfriend out of jealousy. The police pointed out that over a hundred of the couple's love letters were at the crime scene. Why had Dorena brought them to the motor court? Perhaps she intended to break up with Leslie and was going to return them. Investigators found that Dorena had been no more faithful to Leslie than he had been to Mary. Two days before Dorena died, she'd had a date with an Oakland airport employee named John. She seemed depressed during the date and told John that she "had returned a ring to a man and hurt him." She was probably referring not to Leslie but to a third man she had recently been dating, Master Sergeant H. B., who had given her an engagement ring in June. She returned it to the sergeant two weeks before her murder along with a note stating that a man she knew "is pretty desperate and I'm going to give him one last weekend." This, presumably, was Leslie. Only a few hours before her death, Dorena confided to a friend, "I've got a new blond boyfriend. I'm crazy about him." She probably meant John. When these facts hit newsprint, Leslie countered that he had not been jealous and, in fact, had encouraged Dorena to see other men. "They say there were other men. She went out with others, always with my approval. But the more she went out with the others, the more she loved me. That is what she would say."

The third and most romantic theory was that the murder was a suicide pact gone wrong. Perhaps Leslie and Dorena, deeply in love, had realized that their situation was hopeless. He was twice her age, married, and had two children and a very angry wife. Why not just end it all to the strains of "Clair de Lune" and be together forever in the afterlife? The theory goes that after shooting his willing victim, Leslie lost the nerve to shoot himself. Instead, he turned himself in and, having nothing left to live for and feeling ashamed for the grief he'd caused his family, was determined to let the State finish the job for him. Had Leslie admitted that Dorena's death was the result of a botched suicide pact, he likely would have gotten a life sentence. San Quentin's warden, Clinton Duffy, wrote a few years after the case: "It is conceivable that a competent attorney could have gotten him off with a life sentence. The average lifer in California serves about fifteen years, and Leslie would have been young enough to start afresh." But since it was plausible that Leslie had committed the murder out of jealousy, and he refused to reveal his motive, the judge gave him death. It was the verdict Leslie wanted anyway. "I have an appointment, and I will keep it," he told the warden.

Leslie's "appointment" was set for January 22, 1943. He was the only man on Death Row to have such a collection of jewelry and fine clothing. He wrote letters on stationery embossed with the Gireth family crest. He even brought a collection of twenty classical records, but he could not play them since his record player was stored in the prison's property room. His gentleness and good breeding made a lasting impression on the warden, who wrote: "I talked with him many times on the row—about the war, Glendale, his family, prisons, music, art, and other things about which he had considerable knowledge, but when

I asked him about the girl he would turn away and say nothing more. This sparring went on for months, but Leslie refused to reveal why he murdered the girl or why he would not fight for his life." In fact, he asked the warden not to help him win any stays of execution.

Three days before he went to the gas chamber, the prisoner held a news conference in the warden's office in which he asked the reporters to be considerate and understanding when they wrote their accounts of his death. "There are certain things absolutely impossible to explain to people so they would understand. . . . I feel I would be thoroughly misunderstood if I tried to explain." The progress of World War II was also on his mind; he added that he wished to send out "a prayer to God to help our fighting men, so the Stars and Stripes will always fly as proudly as ever." He allowed the news photographers to take pictures of him "looking through the window to the waters of Paradise Cove, and beyond them, to a place he will never know again," to use the *San Francisco Chronicle*'s haunting phrase.

Toward the end, even the estranged wife Mary appealed to the governor to commute the prisoner's sentence. "I am trying desperately to do anything I can to save Leslie for the sake of our two sons," she told the press. "In my opinion the State has not shown that there was any motive whatsoever for the murder of the girl." Of course, the State was hampered by the fact that Leslie refused to speak about the crime, and besides, the prosecution is not required to prove motive. The governor refused to intervene in the due process of the law; the prisoner himself sent a telegram asking him not to. Soon came Leslie's legendary last day on earth.

On the night of Thursday, January 21, Leslie asked the warden if he might be allowed to listen to records on his phonograph. The record player was taken from storage and brought to his cell. He spent the night smoking cigarettes, listening to "Clair de Lune," and asking the warden all the technical details about death by breathing poisonous fumes. When it came time to order a last meal, he asked for two hamburgers and two Cokes.

Later he explained to the warden: "You see, whenever Dorena and I went anywhere—to the beach, or on a picnic, even the night she died—we always had a hamburger and a Coke and our own little phonograph. And last night, well . . . it was just the same as always."

At ten o'clock on the morning of Friday, January 22, Leslie walked to the gas chamber with a firm step as his portable phonograph played Schubert's "Ave Maria," a selection that had also been sung at Dorena's funeral. If nothing else, Leslie knew how to make a dramatic exit. When he sat down in the chair in the chamber, he impatiently helped a guard strap him in. Leslie's hunger for death seemed unaccountable to most people; those who spoke with him in his last hours said that he was convinced he would be reunited with Dorena, and perhaps that is the best explanation we will ever have. Twenty cyanide eggs were dropped into the chamber, releasing lethal gas. Four deep breaths later, Leslie was dead. Dorena was buried in Forest Lawn Memorial Park in Glendale; so was Leslie, but they were not buried together.

After Leslie paid the full penalty of the law, the warden found a note in the dead man's cell, written in beautiful script on his most elegant stationery. "There are times when one can say very little, but these few words I mean in all sincerity: Thank you so much for everything."

An Imperfect Crime

Jacob Charles D., wealthy investor and president of a mining company in Superior, Arizona, disappeared in Los Angeles on August 19, 1920. He turned up on September 23 where he was least expected: buried under cement in a sealed box, down in the cellar at 675 Catalina Street—a new house costing $25,000—property Jacob himself owned. He had been shot through the neck.

When Jacob disappeared, he was occupying a room in the house where he was buried. That particular room had bloodstains and a pistol—one chamber of which contained a bullet of the wrong caliber. It was surmised that someone shot Jacob and then hastily put an incompatible bullet in the empty chamber, hoping to fool detectives into thinking the weapon had not been fired.

During the initial investigation into Jacob's disappearance, Louise Peete, the housekeeper, told searchers that Jacob had "left a month ago." With the discovery of the body in the very house that Louise tended, police knew that wasn't true. They also found that Louise had been tootling around town in Jacob's car. In addition, she had subleased the house to T. T. M., with no apparent authority from Jacob. T. T. M. told the police that when he'd rented the house, the housekeeper had told him the basement was off-limits.

That was when attorney Rush and a detective went to the cellar and in short order made the acquaintance of the missing Jacob, as mentioned above.

They found Louise in Denver. She surrendered, claiming that Jacob had gone away suddenly, leaving his packed bags in the hallway, and the whole thing was a dark mystery to her too. Corpse in the basement? What corpse in the basement?

But detectives discovered that she'd pawned Jacob's diamond ring, and a man named Bill testified that she'd called him asking where she could get cement.

It was all circumstantial evidence, but as that self-righteous bore Thoreau once said, "Some circumstantial evidence is very strong, as when you find a trout in the milk." Louise was considered lucky not to get the death penalty. She first went to San Quentin and later to the California State Prison for Women at Tehachapi.

Flash forward to November 1935. Fletcher W., a Phoenix truck driver, had never purchased anything at auction in his life. But the once grand, now obsolete Union Hotel was about to be torn down, and various odds and ends found in the building were placed on the auction block. Among them was an old trunk that struck Fletcher's fancy. He put in the winning bid of $3.75.

After getting a better-than-average scolding from his wife, Fletcher opened the trunk with a crowbar. It contained yards of velvet, twenty-four pairs of silk hose of such loud patterns that they seemed appropriate for a circus performer, silver slippers, lingerie, evening gowns to which still clung a whiff of perfume, hats mashed flat, trays of jewelry, and a cache of love letters written long ago between a Louise and a Jacob!

Fletcher had no idea who those people were, but he found out after making a few inquiries. He did the gentlemanly thing: he mailed the bundle of letters to Louise via the warden at Tehachapi instead of releasing them to the newspapers.

Gordon's Murder Farm

Gordon Northcott had a tough childhood. His mother was so disappointed when she gave birth to him in 1906 instead of the daughter she wanted that she refused to acknowledge his gender and raised little Gordon as a girl. He was not allowed to wear boys' clothes until he was sixteen. To make matters worse, in adolescence he grew three-inch bristles all over his body, causing the press to dub him "the Ape Boy" when he entered the national stage under unpromising circumstances. His own father called him "an ape man . . . over whom only his mother had complete control." There are those who like to think that Gordon's upbringing, awful as it was, somehow excuses him for everything he did later.

Gordon's parents were Sarah Louise and Cyrus George Northcott—or maybe they were Sarah Louisa and George Cyrus; their names vary in press accounts. They moved from Ontario to Los Angeles in 1923 with Gordon; their daughter Winnifred appears not to have moved with the family and remained in Canada. City life did not agree with young Gordon, even if his mother did permit him to dress like a boy there, and in 1926 Cyrus Northcott moved his family to a chicken ranch five miles southeast of Wineville, Riverside County, off of Etiwanda Boulevard. Cyrus wanted to "get the boy away from the city." The experiment was not a success. Around Christmas 1927, Cyrus abandoned his family and moved back to Los Angeles. He later claimed that he had feared for his life. More likely, he decided that it was easier to leave than to tell the police what he knew about his son's distasteful hobby. For several months, the only residents at the ranch—to be precise, the only ones who stayed there for any length of time—were Gordon, his mother, and a fifteen-year-old relative from Canada, Sanford C. The Northcotts seemed destined to live out an obscure (though dysfunctional) family life until they became the center of events that would horrify the nation, at least until its attention was diverted by fresher horrors.

Wineville was a quiet place in 1928. The only real excitement the community knew for months occurred when two brothers from Pomona disappeared on May 16: Louis and Nelson W., aged twelve and ten respectively, last seen wearing their Boy Scout uniforms. The police performed a wide search aided by citizens and the brothers' fellow Scouts. Fears were relieved on May 19 when Louis and Nelson's parents received a letter with a Pomona postmark from the boys, in which they stated that they had decided to travel to Mexico on a whim. A handwriting expert examined the letter and declared that Louis had definitely written it. On May 28 came another letter, this time postmarked Corona, in which the brothers claimed to be sleeping in the daytime and "bumming" their way through the country at night: "We are having a grand time." But after a few months the boys had not returned home and had ceased all communication with their parents. Their mysterious disappearance was the talk of the community for a few days then became a matter of secondary interest to everyone but the boys' parents.

In August, Gordon and his family received a visitor from Canada: Jessie C., the nineteen-year-old sister of their young boarder Sanford. He told her disturbing secrets when they found some time away from the watchful and malevolent eyes of Gordon and his mother who, growing suspicious, soon booted Jessie off the premises. Undaunted, Jessie told the police that Sanford had been living on the family's ranch for some time in violation of immigration laws. The authorities came to the farm on August 31 and took the gaunt youth to a Los Angeles detention home. It was the luckiest day of his life. He gratefully told the police that in 1926 he had been kidnapped from his home in Saskatchewan by his relatives and made a prisoner at their chicken farm. There he was beaten and sexually abused by Uncle Gordon, whom he knew to have abducted, molested, tortured, and murdered at least three boys.

Sanford told the police that the first victim was an unnamed Mexican about eighteen years old, who was murdered horribly on or around February 2, 1928. Sanford did not witness the slaying and thought that it had occurred away from the ranch "but knew that it had been done after Gordon had subjected [the Mexican] to a week's torture," as the *New York Times* put it. The young man was shot and beheaded. Gordon bundled the headless corpse into his car and dumped it on the highway at Puente, but for some unknowable reason he took the head back to the chicken ranch in a pail. There he burned it, smashed it with an ax, and tossed the charred fragments in a dump.

The next victim came in March. Gordon introduced him as a playmate named Walter C., whom Sanford deduced was a mentally defective nine-year-old boy who had been in the news after disappearing from his home in Los Angeles. "For a week ... Walter was subjected to frightful tortures while tied to a bed," related the *Times*. (The papers were circumspect in describing what exactly Gordon did to his victims, but we are given to understand that it was very, very bad.) He wanted to shoot Walter, but his mother was afraid that he would get caught if he employed such a noisy method. She performed her motherly duty by killing Walter herself with an ax on March 16.

Then on May 16, Gordon came to the ranch with two boys in his car. At the Los Angeles police headquarters, Sanford saw photographs of the missing brothers Louis and Nelson and identified them as the boys Gordon had for ten days "put through tortures similar to those meted out to Walter and the Mexican." When Gordon tired of his captives, he murdered one of the boys with an ax and then forced Sanford to help kill the other. Sanford claimed that he was also coerced into helping bury the bodies in shallow graves within fifty yards of the ranch's chicken house.

It was a gruesome and detailed story, but was it true? Sheriff Clem S. had reason to be skeptical at first. The police claimed that Walter was alive and at the Los Angeles County institution for the feeble-minded at Norwalk. The police said he had been found in Illinois weeks before and returned to his mother, Christine—but she denied that he was her son. It might seem strange for the police to take the position that the mother didn't know her own son, but they believed her identification might have been faulty due to mental illness as she had spent time in the county hospital's psychopathic ward. Later, after a serious miscarriage of justice, Christine was proved correct. (This extraordinary circumstance was dramatized in Clint Eastwood's 2008 film *Changeling*.) In addition, N. H. W., father of the missing brothers, was sure his sons were alive. Reverend L. L. M. of the First Church of Christ, Riverside, told the press that he'd spoken with the boys in Oklahoma in August.

After a cursory search, the police found burned bones scattered about the ranch, but they appeared to be the remnants of chickens rather than humans. On the other hand was this instructive fact: Gordon and his mother had fled to Canada on September 1, the day after the authorities had picked up Sanford, leaving the sixty-two-year-old father behind in Los Angeles.

Upon closer investigation, the authorities found evidence backing up Sanford's nightmarish tale. The reverend's story did not hold water; because the disappearance of the brothers had been highly publicized, he was asked why he did not tell their father of the sighting at the time, rather than waiting three months to tell his tale to the Los Angeles newspapers. He gave no explanation and admitted that he could not give a clear description of the appearance of the boys he'd seen in Oklahoma. In the end, the minister seemed to be mistaken at best, a publicity hound at worst. More stimulating from an investigative point of view, the headless body of a young male had indeed been found recently at Puente. There was a .22-caliber rifle bullet just below his heart, and a .22 rifle was discovered at the ranch. A gunnysack found at the ranch had the same serial number as the gunnysack that was wrapped around the torso of the decapitated youth. Police found a bloodstained cot in a henhouse and a bloody ax. Even the cellar steps were stained with blood. Scattered across the three acres of the chicken farm were human hair and enough human bones to fill eight large jars. Among the bones, paleontologists identified fragments of an ankle, leg, and skull. One piece of a skull still had a lock of blond hair clinging to it. The scientists also found two complete pelvises, the kneecap of a small boy, a number of finger bones in quicklime, and soil stained with a quantity of human blood. The authorities arrested the father on suspicion of murder on September 15.

Cyrus Northcott folded after five hours of questioning. He admitted that Sanford's story was true; he knew because his son had boasted of his sadistic crimes. "I had nothing to do with it," he told the police, "although I knew that three boys were killed there. . . . I was never at the farm when anything like that was going on. I moved into the city and wanted to be away from it all." He expressed a mortal fear of his wife and son. The pitiable Cyrus was guilty only of cowardice and of not coming forward when he knew the others were up to something. He was held in the detention ward of the Riverside County hospital as a material witness, along with Sanford. It was noted that while in custody, the youth transformed from sullen and frightened to "cheerful and like any other lad of his age," but he and his relative Cyrus refused to speak to each other.

Plentiful evidence indicated that awful deeds had transpired on the farm, but there was still little proof that Sanford was correct about the identities of the victims. The police insisted that Walter C. was alive and the father of the missing brothers, grasping at straws, continued to believe that his sons were in Mexico. On September 18, the Riverside County district attorney decided that he had proof enough to formally charge the missing Gordon and his mother with murder.

The next day, Canadian police captured Gordon Northcott at Okanagan Landing, near Vernon, British Columbia. In an exquisitely cinematic moment, a ferryboat operator was reading a newspaper account of the young man's crimes and recognized the suspect boarding his craft from a photograph accompanying the article. The youth made himself all the more conspicuous by paying his fare with an American hundred-dollar bill. The operator immediately alerted the Mounties. On the same day, Gordon's mother was seized at Calgary, Alberta. For thirty hours, she insisted she was "Mrs. J. Black," pathetic childless widow, but she confessed after learning that her son had also been arrested. The police continued to search for two missing women related to the suspects whom they feared had been murdered for knowing too much: Gordon's niece Jessie C., who had disappeared from sight after her visit to the ranch back in August, and Winnifred, Gordon's older sister and the mother of his accusers, Sanford and Jessie. The Mounties soon located Jessie but kept her location secret. Winnifred was found alive and well in Calgary on September 21.

Around the time mother and son were arrested came conclusive proof that the missing brothers Louis and Nelson had been at the farm. Their belongings turned up there, including a whistle and Boy Scout badges. The boys were in the habit of making toy boats, and a piece of wood showed the outline of a boat drawn in pencil. (Sanford confirmed that the youngsters had occupied themselves while being held captive by attempting to make a toy boat.) Investigators found a burned homemade banjo, an instrument known to have been made by the missing boys, and banjo keys at the boys' previous residence matched it perfectly. In a chicken coop, police discovered a book about model airplanes that had been checked out by the boys at the Pomona library. A flyleaf was torn out, and it was determined that the first letter the boys had sent to their parents had been written on the missing page. Gordon had forced the boys to write the letters before he'd murdered them to suggest they were alive and wandering the Mexican countryside.

Gordon fully appreciated the difficulty of his situation. During extradition hearings, he sneered at detectives when they told him they had evidence that he'd murdered the brothers Louis and Nelson W., but his demeanor changed instantly when Sanford's affidavit was read aloud. A reporter described the scene: "He asked to see the signature on the affidavit, and paled visibly as he appeared satisfied that Sanford had really signed the evidence against him." Gordon realized that his only hope was to sow seeds of reasonable doubt in public opinion via the newspapers, a trick that has worked wonders for many a killer before and since. He denied having committed the murders ("What awful things they say about a man!"), declared that his father and nephew were both insane, and swore he would fight extradition to the United States on the grounds that "we need roads and bridges in Riverside County, not ridiculous yet expensive criminal trials." When reporters asked why he'd fled to Canada if he was innocent, Gordon lamely replied that it was to protect his mother: "I simply could not tell her of what they were accusing me. I kept it all from her, newspapers and everything. I wanted to get her away to a safe place, then come back alone and fight this thing."

He was able to stave off the inevitable until November 7, when Vancouver's extradition court ruled that he would have to stand trial in California. At some point, the Riverside authorities realized that the boy in the institution for the feeble-minded was not Walter C., so Gordon and his mother faced charges of murdering Walter, the brothers, and the still unidentified Mexican youth. Gordon was also charged with having performed against Sanford an "infamous crime," the exact nature of which was discreetly left untold in the newspapers.

(The press's cautious descriptions of the captured "Ape Boy's" sexuality are of passing interest as a mirror of the times. Reporters and police did not openly call him a homosexual, though the then-common euphemisms "pervert," "effeminate," and "degenerate" were employed with the unstated conviction that worldly newspaper readers would read between the lines. Sometimes other hints were dropped with more or less subtlety. Journalists noted that he was womanishly fastidious in his dress, sometimes describing the "dude's" apparel right down to the bright colors of his ties and handkerchiefs. A *United Press* journalist mentioned that Gordon's personal idiosyncrasies included speaking with a pronounced lisp in a "high-pitched soprano voice." Another report noted that Gordon inspired "some disgust from police and newspapermen" by his constant use of colorless lipstick. On one occasion a deputy sheriff remarked, "Gordon is a killer, no doubt, but hanged if he doesn't look and act more like a female impersonator.")

While on the train from Canada to Los Angeles, the heavily guarded Gordon told reporters that he had been framed and unctuously quoted the Scriptures: "Father, forgive them, for they know not what they do." He felt certain the case would never come to trial, adding with sublime but misplaced confidence that he could clear up everything with just a few statements. He replied to reporters' questions with peevish sarcasm, insincere religiosity, and non-answers.

"Then you did not kill the Mexican boy and haul his body to Puente?" asked one journalist.

"No. I'm not a hearse driver."

"Did you ever hire a Mexican boy on your ranch?"

"I won't discuss that matter. It isn't to the point, anyway. All ranches in Southern California have some Mexican workers."

"Do you have faith in your religion to carry you through this?"

"Absolutely. In this day and age a person cannot be too religious—too close to Christ."

"Where were you born, and where were you educated?"

"That's another question I must decline to answer."

"Would you plead guilty to all the murders to save your mother?"

"We have justice in this state, and I think such martyrdom would be uncalled for."

"Do you expect to deny or affirm any press reports in the future?"

"This will be my last statement to reporters. I think they're unfair and I have a natural repulsion for morbid news. The place for such matters is in the court."

"Why do you dislike meeting reporters?"

"Because they don't write the truth. They write anything to make a good story. I have a message for them, too, but I'll bet you won't print it."

"What is that?"

"'Judge not, that ye be not also judged.'"

(Of course, Gordon was not above using the hated press to try to gain sympathy from the public by posing as a hounded, befuddled innocent whose ranch just happened to be liberally adorned with human blood, body parts, and memorabilia from missing boys. Despite his complaints that the press made up stories about him, assistant district attorney Earl R. later complimented the press for its fairness in "refraining from publishing untruths and sticking to the facts of the case as it has developed.")

But despite Gordon's display of derision and braggadocio, before the train reached its destination he broke down and cried for hours. Before the assistant district attorney, an investigator, and Los Angeles policemen, he freely admitted killing the Mexican, adding that the head would never be recovered. He claimed that he'd picked up the boy near Escondido and hired him to work on the ranch. The murder occurred over disputed wages. He asserted also that Sanford helped commit the crime—whether under duress or not, he did not say. He displayed criminal cunning when asked why he had transported the body all the way to Puente: "It was logical, wasn't it, to get it as far away as possible? Besides, there are lots of Mexicans living there." Despite his vow never again to speak to reporters, as soon as he was in L.A., he complained to the press about the United States in general, roundly criticizing the nation's "vulgar" customs in terms that no doubt won him some measure of approbation from the intellectuals of the Twenties, who like their counterparts today, never hesitated to lend a glad ear to anyone who had something negative to say about America.

On the evening of December 3, Gordon voluntarily wrote a confession admitting that he had murdered the Mexican boy, whom he identified as Alvin G. (The identification must not have been confirmed, as later articles continue to refer to the victim as "unknown.") Gordon also promised in writing that he would plead guilty the next day when arraigned in Riverside County on charges of murdering Walter, the brothers, and the Mexican.

But he changed his mind. In the morning, before court met, he led officers on an expedition through the Mojave Desert, promising he would guide them to the remains of his Mexican victim's skull. During the fruitless search, he said studiedly maniacal things, such as "I could not stand to see them killed without first having them make their peace with God. That is why I built the altar at the ranch. I always made them pray. I wanted to be sure the little darlings would go to heaven. . . . Believe me, officers, that chicken ranch was a regular butcher shop." Despite the pretense to wickedness and knowledge of dark secrets, in court later that day he entered a plea of not guilty. On the night of December 4, Gordon again led the authorities on a futile search in the Mojave for remains. During the evening, he claimed he had murdered nine persons; later he changed his tally to seven, and later still he made it eleven. Several times Gordon would stop the motorcade by crying, "There it is!" The police would get out, dig, and find nothing. After a long night of being repeatedly hoodwinked, they noticed that the prisoner wore a "satisfied smirk." There was speculation that Gordon's contradictory statements and actions were only a sham to make plausible an insanity defense.

Gordon's mother, Sarah, arrived in Riverside from Canada on December 8, having protested her innocence all the way. She told the jailers that she was unsure of the year she was born but thought she was "about sixty-one years old." Later she claimed to be fifty-eight. In stark contrast to her son's finely cut, modish clothing, Riverside reporter Jessica Bird noted that Sarah was clad in a rumpled gray coat, an "unbecoming" gray hat, a dress that "appeared somewhat the worse for constant wear," and cheap black shoes.

Reporter George Rix had previously referred to Gordon's "carefully parted" hair; the killer's mother, according to Bird, made do with hair "cut poorly." Drab mother and dandyish son pled not guilty in Superior Court on December 12. During the proceedings, Sarah was notably better dressed than she had been. However, the reporter commented of her appearance: "It is, for a woman's, a rough-hewn face, seamed and lined and infinitely tired."

While Sarah was in jail, the sheriff's wife showed her many kindnesses. It melted the prisoner's steely resolve. Gordon maintained his fiction of offended innocence until the props were knocked out from under him on the last day of the year: his mother fired her attorney and unexpectedly confessed in court that she'd murdered Walter C., hinting darkly that Sanford had fatally injured the boy before she finished the job. She claimed that she only wanted "to put [him] out of his misery." The judge immediately sentenced her to life imprisonment at San Quentin, remarking that he'd spared her the death penalty only because she was a woman. In response to this awkward turn of events, Gordon sputtered, "She's a fool and she's crazy—but I'm not."

The next day, New Year's Day 1929, the ever-mercurial Gordon told officials that he would confess. He did, but later recanted his confession. The day after she was sent to prison, Sarah, in an effort to save Gordon, confessed to "all of the crimes my son is charged with," but the police and prosecutors knew better.

Like many serial killers, the formerly obscure Gordon began reveling in his sudden infamy. At last he was *somebody*! He told a deputy sheriff, "I like crowds. I want to get all the notoriety out of this that I can." He was delighted when the other inmates at the Riverside County jail arranged a mirror so they could watch him, and he gushed to the jailer: "[I am] getting better publicity than any Hollywood actor. Everybody is reading about me." Nevertheless, he proved to be less than a model prisoner. He was nervous, snappish, and demanding and insisted that he be given an opportunity to exercise out on the street. Prison officials wisely turned down his request.

The prosecution rejected prospective female jurors during the jury selection process because they deemed it improper to allow women to hear Sanford's pending testimony concerning Gordon's revolting crimes. Thus, the final jury consisted of twelve men—one of whom was a chicken rancher, reportedly to the prisoner's amusement. The court must have relented in its efforts to spare the gentler sex's dainty feelings, however; judging from newspaper accounts, women were allowed to watch the proceedings from the sidelines, though not from the jury box.

Chief defense attorney Norbert S. fought hard before the trial began by deploying all the usual tricks: he claimed that Gordon and Sarah had been denied their Constitutional rights and were subjected to a brutal third degree by lawmen, charges that were quickly disproved. It was pointed out, for example, that Sarah did not change her plea to guilty because of cruel treatment but due to the compassion shown her by the sheriff's wife. Norbert challenged the entire jury panel and demanded that all members be discharged from hearing the case, which the judge denied. Norbert requested that an impartial lunacy commission be formed to study his client's mental state, to which the judge agreed. After some changes in personnel, the commission consisted of four expert witnesses: two psychiatrists and two scientists to study forensic evidence. Pushing his luck, Norbert asked for a change of venue to Orange County, which the court refused on the grounds that he had not sufficiently proved that public feeling against Gordon could result in an unfair trial.

In addition to these pleas, Norbert demanded that Sarah Northcott be allowed to attend the trial so she could establish an alibi for Gordon. Norbert was trying to cover all bases by arguing that Gordon hadn't killed anyone—and if he had, he was insane! One wonders exactly why Norbert thought Sarah necessary to his case, since she'd changed her story so many times that her word would seem to be worthless. Though she'd said otherwise earlier, now she maintained that she'd been coerced into signing her confession, a charge denied by the sheriff, his wife, and other witnesses. She was inconsistent, asserting one day that Gordon had not been on the ranch the night Walter was slain and later that he was at home repairing a radio. It was clear that she was willing to swear to anything as long as she thought it might save her wretched son from the gallows. Far too late, she was learning how to be a caring mother.

The avenue to an insanity defense was abruptly closed after the psychiatrists on the lunacy commission examined Gordon and declared him sane on January 10. "It is our opinion that he at the present time fully realizes the difference between right and wrong, and is wholly responsible for all of his conduct," they wrote, though it could have been argued that the matter in question was not Gordon's mental state at present but his mental state at the time of the murders. Even so, it was obvious that Gordon knew right from wrong and had taken careful, even frantic measures to avoid detection and punishment. To make matters worse for the defense, two alienists who had signed affidavits for defense attorney Norbert declaring that they believed Gordon insane refused to swear to the sincerity of their belief in court.

Shortly after the trial began on January 10, the defense attorney made the absurd suggestion that the headless man found near Puente might have been run over by a train. It will be recalled that the head was nowhere to be found and that the body had a bullet wound and was wrapped in a gunnysack. In addition, the nearest railroad tracks were 1,400 feet away from the spot where the corpse was found. In the ensuing days, Gordon had to endure the harrowing testimony of the boys' parents, who had finally accepted that their sons would never again come home. The father broke down on the stand on January 12 as he examined scraps of clothing found at the murder farm: "Those are the shoes I bought for Louis." On the same day, a ballistics expert testified that the bullet found in the unknown man's body could have been fired from a rifle found in the home, though he could not state that the bullet certainly had come from the rifle.

The most eagerly anticipated witness was Sanford, who took the stand on January 14. Reporter George Rix noticed that Gordon's former indifference was replaced by palpable nervousness. "Testimony more damaging than that delivered by [Sanford] . . . seldom has been heard in any court," George wrote. "It was given in low-voiced monosyllables, in the form of answers to queries put by the prosecution, in an atmosphere of electric tension. The drop of the mythical pin could have been heard at any moment during the hour and a half the fifteen-year-old youth was on the stand."

The teenager gave a straightforward account of the degrading treatment he had received at his uncle's hands, of the torture and murder of the brothers, and of the time Gordon showed up with the head of the Mexican youth in a pail. Gordon had freely admitted to Sanford that he'd dumped the Mexican's body near Puente and confided that if he were ever suspected, he had concocted a story about hiring the young man to do some work and having to kill him in self-defense. Sanford estimated that at least ten or twelve other boys had been abducted by Gordon and brought to the ranch, where they were "abused" but not killed. A reporter summarized this portion of the testimony: "The boys would be brought in at night and taken away at night. Their eyes were covered so they could not see, preventing their leading the authorities to the ranch." Sanford told of being forced to dig a grave intended for two of the neighbors whom Gordon planned to invite to the ranch and murder so he could get at their four sons. For some reason, Gordon backed out of this plan, unspeakably evil even by his standards.

At one point during his testimony, Sanford was asked to strip to the waist and show the jurors a number of scars that illustrated the injuries he had received from Gordon, including a burn made by scalding water. Outside of the courtroom, Sanford admitted that he was terrified of testifying against Gordon and feared that if his uncle were given only a life sentence, he might someday be paroled and track him down and kill him.

When it became clear to Gordon that the trial was not going his way, he followed his mother's example by petulantly firing his three defense attorneys on January 16 and representing himself, as fellow serial killer Ted Bundy did when on trial for his life many decades later. But at least Bundy did have some prior legal experience. Gordon ended up proving conclusively the old legal joke: "A man who performs as his own lawyer has a fool for a client." The prosecutors kept up a somber, legalistic façade, but they could scarcely believe their good fortune. The judge allowed the three defense attorneys to remain in the courtroom to provide legal advice in case Gordon found himself in over his head. Gordon got off to a memorable start when, during a court recess, he sneered that only about 5 percent of Sanford's testimony was true. Which 5 percent, he did not say.

While acting as his own attorney, Gordon made what he fancied to be eloquent and heartrending speeches before the jury. He promised that he would subpoena over thirty witnesses to testify in his favor, including his mother and father and his niece, Jessie. Before the proceedings began on January 17, he announced to the media with unbecoming arrogance: "I'll keep Sanford on the witness stand all day, and before I am through with him I'll convince the court and the jury that he is the biggest liar in seven counties." Gordon's boast proved half true: he did cross-examine Sanford but succeeded only in further incriminating himself. He began by acknowledging the part of Sanford's testimony maintaining that Gordon had kept the brothers locked up in the henhouse. If this were true, asked Gordon smugly, why didn't you release them? Sanford's matter-of-fact reply caused his questioner the first of many uncomfortable moments: "You had the key to the henhouse." Afterward, Gordon tried and failed to trip up Sanford as to the time of day he claimed the murders had occurred.

Then there was the matter of the bloody dirt found by investigators. Gordon attempted to explain it away by claiming that it was his own blood; he said he had frequent nosebleeds and rather than employing a handkerchief or tissue as does everyone else in Christendom, he would go outside and let his nose bleed freely onto the earth—yes, even into deep holes in the ground that happened to resemble makeshift graves. He cross-examined Sanford: "Do you recall my having to consult a physician for hemorrhage of the nose?"

"Your nose wasn't bleeding enough that you couldn't stop it with a handkerchief," Sanford countered, and Gordon quickly dropped the subject. After getting Sanford to admit that a dead dog had recently been buried on the ranch, Gordon claimed that the bones found on the premises were actually the remains of the dog, as though skilled forensic experts were unable to tell the difference between human and canine bones.

Abruptly taking a different tack, Gordon demanded: "When I was away from the ranch didn't you have an opportunity to write a letter to your parents?" Sanford sensibly replied that he was afraid to write for help because he never knew when Gordon might return to the farm.

There was more, much more, but those were the highlights. On one detail only did Gordon manage to get Sanford to contradict himself, and it was a point of no possible consequence: Sanford did not know the precise ages of the brothers Louis and Nelson W. The tables were turning most decisively; the predator was being backed into a corner by his erstwhile prey, and reporters noted that the formerly fearful Sanford was more than a match for Gordon. One wrote: "The boy's sharp and decisive answers proved that he had regained his nerve, that the moment of fear that came over him at the start of the examination had passed and that he was equal to the long, drawn-out grill." Under cross-examination Sanford never contradicted any major statements he had made under direct examination, and Gordon's attempt at playing lawyer was an ignominious failure.

The next day, the prosecution placed on the stand a very fortunate boy, eleven-year-old John T., Jr. of Colton, who positively identified Gordon as the man who'd attempted to force him into an automobile at an amusement park in autumn 1927. John Jr. and his father had chased the would-be abductor but failed to catch him. It was a lucky day not only for the boy but for Gordon as well, since John Jr.'s father had a knife and intended to kill

Gordon. Had he succeeded, the lives of four boys (and probably many more) would have been saved. John Jr. and his father were determined to testify against Gordon when they recognized his photo in a newspaper.

When John Jr.'s father took the witness stand, "attorney" Gordon suggested that the witness held a grudge against him since they'd been involved in a minor automobile wreck. The idea was a complete invention. John Sr. had encountered Gordon only once, on the occasion when he chased the latter across the fairgrounds with a knife. Nobody has ever figured out where Gordon got the idea for this novel, but ridiculous, defense.

Next up was Detective Chester L., one of the first investigators on the crime scene. He told of finding empty graves containing quicklime. Under cross-examination, Chester said that Cyrus had brought the lime to the ranch "and that he knew the purpose for which it was to be used." But this admission hardly proved Gordon guiltless and instead harmed his case by getting into the record the implication that his father knew about Gordon's activities—something Cyrus freely admitted anyway.

The next witness, special deputy sheriff Lester G., testified that the family ranch had been under constant guard since the news of the murders broke, and therefore it was impossible for anyone to have planted evidence at the scene. Gordon did not dare challenge Lester's testimony. The State had its turn the rest of the day, and the direct examination of the neighbors whom Gordon had desired to exterminate, according to Sanford, did not bode well for the accused, because they told of finding capsules in peaches served at a meal they'd eaten at the ranch one night. Gordon had originally introduced himself to them as "Mr. Craig," for no discernible reason, while his mother called herself "Mrs. Mayo." That they used aliases made them look guilty of something. The court session ended with Gordon pleading to the judge for permission to consult with the defense attorneys he had so highhandedly fired.

The prosecution was scheduled to bring a plethora of physical evidence found at the chicken farm into court on Monday,

January 21, including pieces of human bone and skin, human hair, a human tooth, bloody door sills from the henhouse, and a boy's cap positively identified by Louis and Nelson's mother as one she had purchased at a local J. C. Penney's store. Many trial watchers wondered how Gordon, acting in his own defense, would fare against such compelling evidence and expert testimony. He answered their question on Monday when he attempted to stop the proceedings by claiming to be sick. Two doctors examined the prisoner and declared that Gordon was faking. The trial continued as scheduled.

While a criminologist and handwriting expert testified concerning the hideous contents of nearly a hundred glass cases full of evidence, Gordon made a point of coughing loudly and piteously from time to time as though to say "See, I really *am* sick!" The handwriting expert demonstrated that the letters to Louis and Nelson's parents had been written by Louis on paper torn from a library book.

Dr. N. of the dental department of the University of Southern California testified that the human tooth found was from a child around ten years old. Gordon could muster only a few "inconsequential questions," according to one newspaper account, and then offered a blanket objection to all of Dr. N.'s testimony. The judge overruled the objection. Gordon "laughingly remarked that it might be a chicken's tooth for all he knew." This was widely interpreted to be a joke of some sort.

Despite his blustering exterior, Gordon was breaking under the strain. Sheriff Clem S. reported on January 22 that Gordon had spent the night crying in his cell. When the accused came to the courtroom that morning, a doctor testified that "his physical condition was such that he would not be able to continue his defense for at least two days." The judge dismissed the court with orders to convene again on Thursday, January 24, but first a paleontologist and a police department chemist testified that the bones, blood, and hair found at the ranch were human.

During the trial's two-day recess, a humbled Gordon acknowledged that he'd made a tremendous tactical error and announced that he would ask the court to reappoint one of the attorneys he'd dismissed. But when he'd fired his attorneys, the court had warned him that if he chose to be his own attorney, he would have to stick to that course of action, sink or swim. Therefore, it came as no surprise when the court turned down Gordon's request, ruling that he must either act as his own attorney to the end of the case or hire a real attorney at his own expense. (The judge did not use the phrase "real attorney," but that is undoubtedly what he meant.) Despite his abysmal track record, Gordon chose to continue to defend himself though his life hung in the balance. The judge allowed Gordon's attorney to remain in court as an advisor, but he immediately damaged Gordon's case further by introducing into evidence what appeared to be forged affidavits.

When court reconvened on January 24, Gordon made a motion that the case be delayed another day, since he wanted more time to examine documents in the possession of his former attorney, Norbert S. The judge refused to burden the court with another delay, noting that it was the defendant's own fault if he had not taken sufficient time to study the evidence. The most important witness of the day was a chemist, who testified in detail that the remains found at the ranch were human. Sanford had claimed that he was forced to wash the bloody ax in a tub of water; the chemist had found traces of human blood on the ax handle and in debris in the bottom of the tub.

The next day Gordon became agitated when the deputy sheriff of Los Angeles County, D. E., took the stand. D. E. had been present when Gordon confessed before the assistant district attorney and other authorities on the train to California, and the prisoner realized that his confession was about to enter the record. He cried "Objection, objection!" repeatedly in his shrill voice. He was overruled every time, and the devastating evidence was permitted. D. E. further testified that "the confession was written voluntarily by [Gordon,] that no promises were made and that he was not intimidated or grilled in any manner." After this testimony, the prosecution rested its case. Contrary to expectations, the State called neither Gordon's father Cyrus nor his niece Jessie to the stand, but observers suspected that they were being held in reserve as rebuttal witnesses.

The defense opened its case on January 28. It had been announced as far back as January 15 that Sarah would be brought from San Quentin to testify in her son's favor, but she arrived too late to take the stand in the court's morning session. Disappointed, Gordon complained that prosecutors were not allowing him to confer with his father, whom he hoped to use as a favorable witness. The assistant district attorney countered that if Gordon had wanted to see his father, he should have followed the process of the law by issuing a subpoena, as it was not the State's policy to allow prisoners to "run all over the country" according to their whims. Instead of Sarah, the defense put on the stand two doctors who had examined the accused in jail after he led police on the futile midnight body search in the desert. Why they were placed on the stand is a mystery, as they had absolutely nothing to say that in any way bolstered Gordon's case. The two doctors were followed by a pair of attorneys; the best they could do was to testify that after the authorities learned of Sanford's presence on the farm in violation of immigration laws, they had not advised Gordon to leave the country—which, of course, he had.

Gordon's niece Jessie took the stand in the afternoon. Gordon placed her under direct examination, and the story she told matched her brother Sanford's testimony "to the minutest detail," in the words of one reporter, who added: "The general impression about the courtroom is that the girl, as a defense witness, turned out to be the best witness for the State." Onlookers wondered what on earth Gordon was thinking when he called her as a witness, but the murderer, full of brag as ever, promised the *Riverside Daily Press*: "[The] sensation of the trial is yet to come. I propose to put mother and [Cyrus] on the witness stand and make them tell the truth. Then I'll go on the stand and tell my own story, and believe me, there will be some fireworks."

As he promised, Gordon put his father, Cyrus, on the stand the next day, January 29. The old man confirmed that his son did have frequent nosebleeds after contracting influenza, though he stopped short of stating that Gordon was in the habit of letting his blood drip into freshly dug five-foot holes in the ground. It did not occur to Gordon that by having his father testify about the nosebleeds, he was tacitly conceding that the blood found on the farm was human. Old Man Cyrus further testified that one scar on Sanford's head was the result of the teenager's accident with an alfalfa cutter and implied that the other scars also were caused by Sanford's "clumsiness." Under Gordon's questioning, Cyrus said that he had never seen Sanford being beaten or otherwise abused and that the boy had appeared satisfied with his lot in life. Cyrus seemed not to consider that Sanford might have been pretending all was well to avoid further punishment. (Another witness, a neighbor named Mrs. G. E., testified that she saw Gordon beat Sanford several times.)

Gordon asked his father if the police had coerced him into saying he was terrified of his son. Cyrus admitted truthfully that he had not been coerced. The best response the embarrassed Gordon could muster was to say sarcastically, "I expected that answer." Then why, one wonders, did he ask?

Sarah took the stand on the morning of January 31. An incidental word about the family's bewildering genealogy: rumor held that Sarah was Gordon's grandmother, and his actual mother was his sister, Winnifred. Cyrus insisted that Sarah was the boy's birth mother and even said so under oath, but Gordon told the *Riverside Daily Press* that Winnifred was his mother and Sanford was therefore his brother—as though that improved matters. During the trial, Sarah claimed under oath on two occasions that she was Gordon's grandmother rather than his mother. The implication was that Gordon was the product of incest between Cyrus and his daughter. On the other hand, it could be that Sarah and Gordon were not above inventing such a story to gain jury sympathy. It would explain their many contradictions on the subject. Winnifred hotly denied that Gordon was her son and provided reporters with the names of the doctor and nurse who had attended his birth. The family tree may be an incomprehensible mystery, but the consensus is that Sarah was the mother and Winnifred was the sister.

Despite Sarah's earlier confession of having murdered Walter C., she now claimed under oath that to her knowledge no murders had occurred on the ranch—*ever*! She revealed that Gordon's accuser Jessie had always hated him. On one occasion in Canada, she alleged, Jessie had attacked Gordon and tried to kill him. Gordon attempted to draw testimony from his mother implying that his cousins, the siblings, were trying to railroad him, but he provoked a salvo of objections from the prosecution "because of the ignorance of the defendant in the proper procedure in examining a witness." At last Gordon lost his temper and the "fireworks" he had promised the media were in full flight. In the words of the local Riverside paper: "Raving and prancing like a caged person he shouted that he would withdraw [Sarah] from the witness stand, go on himself and tell his story of coercion, threats, intimidation, alleged to have been directed at him by officers, including [the district attorney]." If all else fails, claim intimidation; there are plenty of people willing to believe anything they hear about the police as long as it is bad. The State's lawyers responded that he could withdraw Sarah if he wished, but they intended to cross-examine her anyway.

Gordon took the stand that morning. The *Riverside Daily Press* remarked, "The greater part of his testimony was of such a vile nature that it was unprintable." Since he was still defending himself, he would ask himself questions and answer them, a sight that must have seemed to onlookers perilously reminiscent of a vaudeville comedy act. He rambled into irrelevancies so often that the judge had to warn him to stick to the matter at hand. The most significant part of his testimony consisted of unsubstantiated claims that he had been physically abused by the police, including deprivation of sleep and food. He said he was afraid there would be further repercussions against himself and his sainted mother if they testified about the cruel treatment they had received. The judge asked, "Have you seen any indications of [implied] violence?" Gordon admitted he had not. The judge assured Gordon that he and his witness would receive the same protection that is given to any prisoner and witness. His thunder having been most decisively stolen, Gordon calmed down and dropped the police brutality angle. By the time he was finished with the day's deposition, Gordon had wasted the court's time to the tune of five hours, or nearly 50,000 words in the transcript.

Gordon continued his interminable testimony on the morning of February 1. He admitted that he had skipped town after the authorities came to take Sanford away from the ranch but attempted to place an innocent spin on his flight by claiming he was only afraid that he would be jailed for violating immigration policies. He continued to call himself the real victim because his niece Jessie hated him so very much and suggested that she had somehow framed him. (Gordon did not enlighten the court as to how he thought she had collected the fresh body parts of defunct juveniles.) He explained the grave found in the chicken house by claiming he buried dead chickens there, though the only remains found there were those of human boys. The police had found ether at the ranch; Gordon said his mother used it to clean clothes. His nephew, Sanford, had a vivid imagination and was a crime buff and made up all those wild stories after reading in the newspapers about the discovery of the headless Mexican's body and the disappearance of the brothers. Once again, he claimed that the bloody dirt found on the ranch came from his own nosebleeds. Among all of this nonsense, Gordon scored a rare victory when he called as a witness Christine, mother of Walter C., who testified that when she'd met Sanford he had been unable to describe her son—but it will be remembered that she suffered from mental illness.

The State rebutted on Monday, February 4. Under cross-examination, Gordon, Sarah, and Cyrus were very jumpy and agitated whenever the prosecution mentioned the name of Helen W., a supposed acquaintance of the family's and lady friend of Gordon's. It never came to light what knowledge she had of the murders, if any, and why they were so upset when her name was brought into the record. (The judge forced Gordon to name her under oath after the defendant said he didn't want to drag Helen's family into the case. Later an *L.A. Times* reporter testified that he'd overheard Gordon gloating, "I fooled them that time; I lied like hell. That was not her name at all.") Sarah had previously told the assistant district attorney that Gordon's father was an English lord, which she now admitted under oath was a flight of fancy. While on the stand, she said she had five children, but when cross-examined she could not remember their names. In short, she did not come across as a credible witness for the defense.

Probably out of desperation, the next day Gordon called as a character witness a neighbor, Jennie O., who testified under direct examination that "as far as she knew [Gordon's] treatment of [Sanford] was normal." But she let it slip that she had once had a violent altercation with Gordon, who changed the subject fast and doubtless hoped nobody had noticed. But the prosecution did notice, and when cross-examining the witness, the assistant district attorney asked Jennie about that argument. When she was learning how to drive, she said, she'd accidentally run Gordon's car off the road. When she attempted to apologize, he'd called her a liar and threatened to slap her face and wreck her car. Gordon tried to regain ground later that day with his fourth lengthy, pointless cross-examination of Sanford. His acerbic abuse failed to break down Sanford's story, and in the end Gordon was reduced to raving that the witness had been coached.

The final day of testimony came on February 6; the trial had lasted for almost a month, a rare occurrence at that time. It was revealed that Gordon had lied when he'd sworn he was handcuffed to Detective J. H. on the train to California and treated cruelly. In fact, he had been cuffed to Detective Albert K., and Gordon had been permitted to sleep and eat as much as he pleased. Albert even displayed a letter written by Gordon in which the prisoner thanked the detective for his kind treatment. Sheriff Clem S. testified that Gordon had vowed he would lead authorities to the bodies of his victims if he were permitted a private visit with his mother. The visit was arranged, after which Gordon reneged on his promise.

Gordon made a final, maudlin speech to the jury: "The whole case is unreasonable. It's impossible. To do the things they have charged to me, a person would have to be a maniac, and I believe I am sane." Of his nephew's testimony, Gordon said: "It is almost beyond human comprehension that any person should do the things that he has accused me of doing." The reader will note that Gordon did not present evidence that he was guiltless. His defense boiled down to this: it would be impossible for someone to do such awful things; therefore, I could not have done them. He descended to bathos: "Not only am I fighting for my life, but I am fighting also so that I may be free, free to fight again for that little woman [his mother] up in San Quentin." Considering that Sarah had confessed to the ax murder of a little mentally disabled boy, Gordon's attempt to use her imprisonment to play on the jury's sympathy probably seemed a trifle misguided.

Gordon's day of reckoning was February 7. The jury rendered a unanimous guilty verdict. They considered a punishment of life in prison, but, as the *Riverside Daily Press* reported, the members wisely realized that "life imprisonment in California does not mean a great deal." The risk of Gordon's eventually being turned loose by a soft-hearted parole board was too great, so the jury chose capital punishment. The judge sentenced Gordon to death by hanging. Gordon greeted the verdict with a smile and apparently sincere compliments for the judge and jury.

But the day after the verdict was handed down, Gordon amply demonstrated why he deserved no sympathy. Investigators asked him to give directions indicating where the victims' bodies were buried on the now completely abandoned and desolate chicken ranch. He complied, but when the police returned empty-handed, Gordon sneered: "Well, I just had to send you on another wild goose chase before I was through." A couple of days later a mob of 250 men came to the Riverside jail, demanding that Sheriff Clem S. hand over the prisoner so they could have a little chat with him. One caller was N. R. W., father of the murdered brothers. The sheriff talked them into leaving, much to the relief of Gordon, who cowered in his cell, begging the same officers he'd lied to, abused, and sent on wild goose chases to protect him.

Gordon received his official death sentence from the court on February 11. The date was set for April 15, 1929. The prisoner showed none of his former arrogance, telling the judge: "I wish to thank the court for its kind consideration and I wish to thank you . . . I think you are a fair and square judge." Due to appeals, Gordon did not greet the hangman until October 2, 1930.

The night before his execution, Gordon met with the mothers of Walter C. and brothers Louis and Nelson W., who pleaded that he reveal the locations of their sons' graves. The women were only to be the victims of Gordon's final act of sadism. During earlier visits, Gordon had told Walter's mother that he knew nothing whatsoever about Walter's case. This time, he acknowledged that the boy was dead but evasively stated, "Ask my nephew, [Sanford]—or ask my mother. They both know." To Louis and Nelson's mother, he had promised that he would "tell all," but instead, after initially stating that he knew the boys to be dead, he refused to say anything more.

We so often hear of murderers who go fearlessly to their execution that it has almost become a cliché. Gordon was a notable exception in that he set a new standard for Death Row cowardice. According to a prison official, later the warden at San Quentin, on the morning of the hanging Gordon was hysterical in his cell, expressing fear that "the rope would hurt." The guards had to carry him up the gallows stairs. The prison official heard him say, "Say a prayer for me, please," just before the sentence was carried out. Within moments, Gordon received a far more humane and painless death than he'd ever inflicted upon his victims. No one mourned his passing, with the possible exception of his mother.

Gordon left behind a sealed letter in which he blamed all the murders on his father. The district attorney branded it a heartless hoax: "It seems apparent that [Gordon] was making a last effort to do two things—help get his mother out of prison . . . and getting revenge which he thought he should have against his father." One of the dead man's wishes came true. Sarah eventually was paroled and died in Vancouver on February 13, 1949.

Authorities promised Sanford that they would not send him back to the Canadian relatives whom he greatly feared. He became a ward of the court and entered the Whittier State Reformatory where, at last account, he was doing well. Then he dropped from the record and into the murk of history.

Mystery still surrounds the number of Gordon's victims. One gets the impression from the record that he committed many more crimes than were ever discovered. Sanford claimed that bodies were buried within fifty yards of a henhouse; he even led detectives to the places where he insisted the bodies were. The authorities found a number of human bone fragments and two five-foot holes in the ground that exuded a ghastly smell, but complete sets of remains were not found anywhere on the ranch. This probably meant only that when Sanford was taken to the detention center, Gordon had hastily exhumed the bodies and disposed of them permanently before running off to Canada. In fact, the two holes showed signs of having been recently dug up, filled in, and covered with fresh straw. One theory holds that the remains are still waiting to be discovered in the desert surrounding the Morongo Mountains. On many occasions, Gordon drew maps showing mysterious crosses and circles, allegedly marking the locations of secret graves, but all the maps proved to be hoaxes. The final map was made shortly before the execution. Gordon wrote on it, "I am not guilty. If you look here you will find what you want." It proved to be without merit, as had all the other maps. Likely Gordon was having fun at the police's expense from beyond the grave. "As far as I am concerned," said Sheriff Clem S., "the . . . case is closed forever."

Gordon's mother admitted murdering one boy, and Gordon had killed at least three. But his niece, Jessie, estimated that he'd murdered eleven boys within five years, and Sanford thought that possibly as many as fifty boys had been brought to the chicken ranch never to be seen again. Authorities unsuccessfully attempted to link many missing boys to the depraved farmer. A few names that turned up in the press included a Japanese boy named Yamashak; Phillips G., a San Diego Catholic schoolboy; a thirteen-year-old named Nicholas E., whose mutilated remains were found near San Diego, a city Gordon was known to have frequented; and fourteen-year-old Lloyd L. of Glenavon, missing since September 1926. Gordon was even suspected of murdering a couple of adults for a change of pace: a miner at Saugus and a thirty-three-year-old bootlegger named Tony S., who disappeared after visiting the family and whose bullet-riddled car was found only thirteen miles from the ranch.

Nobody knows how many children ceased to exist due to ill-fated chance encounters with Gordon, but his influence also brought an end to Wineville, California. The case brought so much unwanted notoriety that in 1931 the town changed its name to Mira Loma.

A San Diego Serial Killer?

Ten-year-old Virginia B. went missing from her San Diego home on February 11, 1931. Her parents were convinced she had been kidnapped. Their conviction was not based on any real evidence but rather on the fact that that particular crime was much in the news at the time. The police thought Virginia might have drowned in a pool while walking to school, but they rounded up and questioned several known "degenerates." By February 15, the search for the missing child included five hundred adults and five hundred Boy Scouts, who unearthed not so much as a particle of a clue.

George M., a goat herder, found the missing girl's body on Camp Kearney mesa, ten miles from San Diego, on March 10. After seeing her body, deputy coroner Dave G. remarked, "It was the work of a madman." Virginia's injuries were the stuff of nightmares: she had been beheaded, her body wrapped in a burlap potato sack, and both legs were broken. Her skull was so clean of flesh that investigators wondered if the murderer had dunked her head in acid after beheading her. Her arms and head had been removed with surgical precision, leading some to believe her killer was an insane surgeon. Her coat and library books were nearby, confirming the body's identity. The only viable clue was tracks made by unfashionably narrow automobile tires, "balloon-style" car tires being popular in 1931.

Was Virginia murdered on the mesa? Moldy leaves in the sack suggested that she had been buried elsewhere, then exhumed, wrapped in the bag, transported to the mesa, and dumped.

On March 17, a letter signed "The Doctor" was left under the door of a San Diego gas station. The police took it seriously without saying why—perhaps an unexpurgated version included facts only the murderer could have known—but the letter as released to the press sounds unmistakably like the work of a crank: "I killed Virginia. I have performed a perfect crime. I am no degenerate. She did not suffer. You will never find me, for I left no clue. It proves I am superior."

The murder of the little girl remains unsolved, but at the time it recalled to Californians two horrifying recent cases: during the 1927 Christmas season, sadistic young kidnapper William Hickman had abducted, murdered, and mutilated twelve-year-old Marian Parker of Los Angeles in a similar manner. The mesa where Virginia was found was the same place where serial killer and chicken rancher gone wrong Gordon Northcott had deposited the body of one of his many victims, a Mexican boy. But neither William nor Gordon was responsible for murdering Virginia, they having been hanged on October 18, 1928, and October 2, 1930, respectively.

On or around April 16, 1931, someone strangled forty-three-year-old Mrs. W. B. ("Diamond Dolly"), a racetrack aficionado, in her San Diego apartment. Her body was not discovered for several days. A man named Henry Y. was arrested in Uniontown, Pennsylvania, and held on suspicion. He was eventually turned loose, and the case remains unsolved. Diamond Dolly's home was ransacked, so possibly her murder was the outcome of a simple burglary.

Late on the night of Saturday, April 18, 1931, twelve-year-old Fred C. of National City told San Diego police he had seen a woman bound and gagged in the back seat of a sedan. Officers took him seriously and established a frantic—but unsuccessful—dragnet to locate the car and the woman.

The next day, picnickers at Black Mountain near La Mesa found the nude body of seventeen-year-old Louise T., a five-and-dime store clerk, hanging from an oak tree limb. She had been dead at least twelve hours. Her slayer had thrown a rope over the tree limb, pulled her body upward, and tied the other end to a stump fifteen feet away. Cause of death appeared to be a combination of a blow to the head and strangulation. Her feet touched the ground, so either Louise was already deceased when suspended or the rope had stretched overnight and lowered her body to the ground.

Various articles were abandoned nearby: a fur-trimmed coat, a light dress, a clerk's smock, new lingerie, an army blanket, and a package containing a brassiere and stockings, which were proved to have been purchased in San Diego on the day of Louise's murder.

An autopsy revealed that Louise had not been sexually assaulted and that human skin was under her fingernails, indicating that she'd fought her attacker vigorously. Detectives must have been elated at first: that Louise had all that clothing with her at the time of her death, including new underwear, suggested that she knew her murderer. All they had to do was track down her known male acquaintances and see which one had recent scratches!

The problem was that Louise was popular with men—*very* popular. When authorities picked her little brown diary's lock and read its contents, they found that she had undertaken "more dates than any girl in town," as the police put it, including some with men who were married or engaged. Their names were withheld from the press to spare innocent men embarrassment—men innocent of murder, anyway. One of her former coworkers, Blanche, thought that Louise was secretly married to a sailor or marine. (Perhaps significantly, she had been hanged with a double half-hitch, a kind of knot one might expect a sailor to be familiar with.) Blanche thought Louise's many dates with different men were a smokescreen to prevent her father from finding out she was married.

Local photographer and retired navy man Harold N. was arraigned for distributing pornographic pictures—some of which were "art photos" of Louise posing in a glade.

Sheriff Ed C. questioned so many men in Louise's life, more than twenty, that he theorized she had been murdered and hanged by a jealous woman. There was a brief flurry of excitement several months later when a sixteen-year-old Los Angeles burglar and navy deserter named Lowell B. confessed to the murder on September 30. However, Lowell was a liar: upon questioning, he was unable to remember whether he'd left his victim clothed or unclad, a detail one would think hard to forget.

On the night she died, Louise wrote a note to her father stating that she was fed up with her home life and intended to move away from San Diego. Did her determination to leave have anything to do with her murder? No one ever found out.

Barely had Louise been laid to rest when San Diego again faced the horror of a brutal unsolved murder. On May 2, twenty-two-year old telephone operator Hazel B. was found dead and fully clothed in Balboa Park's Indian Village, an adobe structure constructed in 1915 as a temporary dwelling for Yuma Indians but which in 1931 served as headquarters for the Boy Scouts. Two Scouts found her under shrubs in an open part of the building called the council chamber. An autopsy showed that Hazel had been stabbed seventeen times, including six times in or near the heart. Like Louise, she had not been raped.

Hazel's parents, Mr. and Mrs. C. A. B., were quick to blame her former boyfriend, thirty-seven-year-old railroad commissary clerk Moss G., who turned himself in when he got wind the police were seeking him. He admitted that on the night of the murder he'd walked Hazel home from a theater and their path had led them through Indian Village to her front door. He swore he left her at the family house; if true, her slayer must have been surveilling the couple and moved in for the kill after Moss walked away.

Hazel had reneged on a promise to marry Moss, and her last boyfriend, a sailor from the U.S.S. *California*, said that Moss had threatened to kill her and commit suicide only a week before. Moss tearfully maintained his innocence even after officers allowed him to gaze upon her corpse. (He kissed her forehead and called her "sweetheart.")

At the inquest, Hazel's fifteen-year-old sister, Edith, testified that Hazel had once confided to her, "I am afraid to quit going with [Moss]. He is the type of man who might kill me."

Things got warmer for Moss when a man and woman who claimed to have been sitting in a car at Balboa Park on the night of the murder said they saw a man leaving the park a few hours before the Boy Scouts found the body. Their description, which they gave before seeing Moss in person, matched him perfectly. He was arrested on May 11.

When Moss went on trial in July, two of the victim's family members testified as to his jealous streak and threats against Hazel. Her mother testified that that was the reason Moss had come immediately to mind when Hazel's body had been found. Despite having an anger management problem, Moss was acquitted by the jury on July 31. He immediately claimed that the police had "suppressed evidence that might have led them to the real murderer" and filed a lawsuit against the San Diego Police Department for $50,000.

The identity of Hazel's killer was never determined.

When seven-year-old Dalbert, the son of Mrs. and Mrs. George A., went missing on July 18, 1933, San Diegans were on edge. They were reminded of the recent kidnapping and murder of Virginia B. When the boy's remains turned up in San Diego Bay on July 24, autopsy surgeons determined that he had been abused even worse than Virginia. He had been "tortured to death," meaning "the boy's ears, eyes, tongue and lips were missing and the body had been mutilated further." These mutilations had been performed while Dalbert was still alive.

Three days later, a man lured two boys into his car and showed them pornographic photos. Alarmed, they abandoned the car but wrote down the license number. The police soon had a man named Basset C. in custody. His home yielded a rusty knife, a stained blanket, and child pornography. Basset appears to have been a decidedly creepy fellow, but there was no solid proof he was a killer.

On August 2, Phillip E., a recent graduate of San Diego High School, confessed to Los Angeles police that he had mutilated and murdered Dalbert. He was arrested and taken to San Diego. Two days later, Phillip made a second confession: his story was a lie that he had concocted in the hope it would help launch his vaudeville career! All it launched for Phillip was a conviction for obstructing justice with a false confession, the punishment for which was five years in jail, a $5,000 fine, or both.

Dalbert's horrifying murder was never solved.

No sooner had San Diego recovered when another body was found in the bay on October 15. Like Dalbert, the body was grossly mutilated; like Virginia, it was dismembered and concealed in a sack, a canvas sailor's bag. Police determined the victim to be sixty-year-old wealthy widow Laura Ellen S. based on her jewelry, which neighbors recognized. She had been struck six times in the head. Her home contained a bloody bed, a bloodstained hammer and hatchet, and a saw with flesh on its blade. An autopsy indicated that like Dalbert, Laura Ellen had been mutilated alive: according to a doctor, Laura Ellen "was unconscious but still alive when her legs were amputated."

A name stenciled on the sea bag—"F. B. Henke, U.S.N."—seemed at first a promising clue, but Henke proved he had been in Ohio on the day of the murder. He said he had given the bag to a friend but could not remember his name.

The top suspect was Thomas J., a forty-year-old ex-convict acquaintance of Laura Ellen's. The papers say nothing more of

Thomas, so evidently he was either never found or provided a solid alibi.

On March 4, 1934, the body of an unnamed young woman was left by the side of a Camp Kearney mesa road near the site where Virginia's body had been abandoned in 1931. The victim was described as "about twenty-five years old, a pretty brunette, wearing a new dress, shoes, and stockings. She wore a gold wedding ring." She had been poisoned.

On August 18, 1934, sixteen-year-old Celia C., the attractive daughter of Mexican customs broker Edward C., was found raped and strangled. Bizarrely, her clenched hands held rabbit hair. She had told her parents she was going for a walk at eight o'clock the previous night—her younger sister, Esther, had considered joining her but decided she was too tired. When Celia did not return home by midnight, her parents sounded the alarm. Police spent several hours looking all over the city for Celia, but at dawn two officers found her dead in her own backyard.

An old trunk found a few feet from the body bore no fingerprints. Celia's murder, like the others, was never solved.

Mrs. Florilla C., age sixty-three, told her neighbor Mattie: "If my shades remain drawn for a day and a half, come over. I'll be dead." Her prognostication came true on March 26, 1938, when Mattie noticed the shades were down on Florilla's Orange Beach cottage, went inside, and found her friend dead on the kitchen floor with one ear nearly torn off. Police determined that she had been beaten to death with a piano stool and had put up a violent struggle for her life. Investigators decided that the motive was robbery—Florilla's purses had been emptied—and that the murder had no connection to the incidents that had terrified the city for the past seven years. But for all that, the murder went unsolved. And then there was the matter of Florilla's eerie prediction of her own demise. Were all these murders unrelated, or was San Diego the hunting grounds of a particularly vicious, never identified Depression-era serial killer who appeared to be experimenting with different methods of killing?

Hollywood Murder Mystery

Had King David Gray been a movie star, his death would be remembered today as one of Hollywood's great mysteries. Instead he was an assistant cameraman at Universal Studios, so his murder caused only a temporary splash.

King, forty-two, was found dead in his car on June 30, 1938, parked in front of the Hollywood post office on Wilcox Avenue. Whoever had shot him in the chest had plenty of nerve. The murder was committed in the most public place imaginable, a site passed by hundreds of people a day. He had been dead between six and ten hours. He was not a suicide, since there was a .32 caliber cartridge on the car floor but no gun. The motive was not robbery; King had a valuable watch, a diamond ring, and $63 in his wallet. A partially empty bottle of wine was in the car.

King's friends described him as "quiet, retiring, and timid." He was a true motion picture industry pioneer, having worked as a head cameraman since 1916; for unknown reasons, however, he spent the last year of his life as an assistant. His friends could think of no one who wanted him dead. Myrtle, the widow, was equally mystified. King had no known enemies; she had last seen him at nine o'clock on the night of his murder. He'd left the house with a friend. Police found that he'd gone straight to the studio, but after that his movements were unaccounted for. Later they discovered that after King had left Universal, he'd attended a party with a man and two women.

The police found a note near King's hand that cast doubt upon the perception of him as a solid family man. Written in a feminine hand, the letter's contents were mundane, but the salutation and closing were surprisingly intimate:

> *Daddy Dear: Everything is quiet here. Please forward my trunk, marked with white chalk to San Souci, Canada. That is a camp on Georgian Bay, near Midland City. It will cost about $9.50—please check it, and thanks to you very much. What are you going to do on the Fourth?*

> There is nothing doing here. I am still praying to be with you soon. Love always, Babe.

King had a secret mailbox at the post office. Perhaps he'd been shot moments after retrieving a love letter?

The author of the note was Frances B. of New Castle, Pennsylvania, who described herself as "a friend of the [King] family." That came as news to Myrtle. Frances was a twenty-nine-year-old former student at the University of Southern California. She said she knew nothing about the murder and had been at home in New Castle since May 27. When Captain H. J. W. identified and questioned the people who'd attended the party with King on the night he died, they also said they could shed no light on the mystery.

The police lab took a closer look at King's car and found a man's shoeprint that didn't match King's shoes. Said the chemist on July 3, "The print is clear and obviously was made near the approximate time of [King's] death. The shoe that made the print can easily be identified, and the man wearing the shoe was either the killer or had vital information." When investigators discovered that "family man" King had been posing as a bachelor, they theorized that the cameraman was murdered by a jealous man over an affair. Others thought him the victim of an aborted holdup, although nothing of value had been taken.

On July 7, police found a .32-caliber automatic pistol abandoned in a vacant lot ten blocks from the post office. It had been wiped clean of fingerprints. A ballistics test showed that it was the murder weapon.

And there matters stand, probably forever. The murder of King was never solved. Interestingly, however, a similar murder occurred several months later. On December 28, 1938, Weldon ("Big Bill") Irvin was shot to death in his car only six blocks from the spot where King was slain. Like King, Weldon's body sat in the car for several hours until it was noticed by a passerby. Weldon was a noted gambler and bookmaker; police said he was murdered due to a "gambling quarrel." Is it possible someone had ordered a hit on Weldon back in June and the assassin had shot King by mistake?

Death of the Party

A pre-Halloween costume party—complete with a live band—was held at the deluxe Valley Country Club Apartments at 15353 Weddington Street in Van Nuys on October 29, 1967. Thirty-one-year-old Kenneth L. was a guest. Described variously as a business directory publisher, a salesman, an advertising executive, and a "loan shark," he sat on a couch in the lobby with a young woman.

A stocky man appeared at the lobby doors and gestured for Kenneth—who appeared not to recognize him—to follow him. When Kenneth approached, the man produced a .38-caliber handgun, which witnesses assumed was a toy, and fired three shots. (There was contradiction concerning the exact circumstances of the shooting. Some witnesses later claimed that a panicked Kenneth had burst into the lobby pursued by his killer.) Two bullets entered Kenneth and the other hit a wall. Then the stocky man fled the building. Kenneth hit the marble floor and did a most convincing impersonation of a dying man, or so the amused two hundred revelers thought.

One guest explained, "It looked to everyone like a skit. When the man fell down and was moving and mumbling on the floor we all thought, gee, this guy is really putting it on." The band, getting into the mood of things, puckishly changed from a fast dance number to a slow dirge. Another partier, aspiring actress Patricia S., recalled that one guest danced around the body.

Kenneth lay on the floor several minutes before a girl said, "I see blood coming out of his mouth."

"It must be a capsule he has in his mouth," said her companion. At last a partygoer examined Kenneth and shouted, "He has no pulse. This man is dead!" Attendee Gale C. remembered, "There was just quiet, shock, and disbelief. Everyone walked around in a daze. It was late and we'd all been drinking and it was hard to grasp what happened." No one recognized the shooter.

Strangely, Kenneth's rental car, which was found in an underground parking lot at the apartment, had caught fire. Investigators thought the car had faulty wiring and that the conflagration was unrelated to the murder.

There the matter rested until April 25, 1969, when a thirty-four-year-old auto salesman from La Crescenta, Jack S., was arrested for the murder. When he went on trial in August, the prosecution claimed the motive was jealousy: Jack had seen his wife, Maria, "dancing erotically" with Kenneth at the party. On September 3, Jack was identified in court as the killer by Bruce C., a partygoer who had stood only fifteen feet away when the shots were fired.

Another witness, James F., testified that he'd heard Jack mutter "I'm gonna go home and get my gun" after seeing his wife's unseemly behavior and that he'd later seen Jack and Maria park at a service station after the shooting and had overheard Maria crying, "You've killed a guy."

The case was far from ironclad. Gale swore the assassin was left-handed; Jack was right-handed. Gale admitted he was astigmatic and had not worn his glasses the night of the party and also that he'd drunk a quarter of a bottle of champagne before the shooting. Defense attorney Robert S. stated that the cause of the murder was the victim's side business in loan sharking. Had Kenneth gotten involved with organized crime? The attorney pointed out that the day after Kenneth's death, a man named Tony A. was murdered in Miami—and Tony had in his possession a check for $10,000 drawn on Kenneth's bank account. The man arrested for killing Tony resembled the general description of the slayer at the party. The defense attorney also claimed that the victim's rental car had been set on fire the night *before* his murder, perhaps as a warning from someone.

Prosecution witness Jay C. testified that Jack had once told him that racketeers had sent him to California to replace Jack "the Enforcer" Whalen, a gangland figure who was shot in a mob hit in Rondelli's, a Sherman Oaks restaurant, on December 2, 1959. Two of Jack's acquaintances testified that he'd admitted that he'd murdered Kenneth but threatened them with death if they told anyone.

The defense presented Jack's father-in-law, Roch D., who swore Jack was at Roch's home in Canoga Park until twenty minutes before the shooting. The defense attorney said twenty minutes was insufficient time for Jack to part company with Roch and drive to the Valley Country Club Apartments in Van Nuys. On the other hand, a detective testified that he'd driven from Canoga Park to Van Nuys as a test several times and that the quickest trip took only twenty-one minutes and five seconds. The swiftness or slowness of the trip depended largely, of course, on traffic conditions.

Jack himself testified that the death was a gangland murder, but his theory seemed unlikely since professional hitmen generally do not rub out an intended victim before two hundred potential witnesses when a dark, abandoned alley would afford more privacy.

There was convincing evidence both for Jack's guilt and for his innocence, but on October 30, 1969—Halloween season!—the jury reached a guilty verdict. Jack was sentenced to life in prison. His conviction was reversed on appeal in 1971 due to errors made during jury instruction, and the case was restored to the Superior Court calendar. Jack wanted witnesses' identification of him in a police lineup thrown out as evidence on the grounds that he considered the circumstances unfair—he was a Caucasian, but most of the men in the lineup were Hispanic. The motion was denied on May 31, 1972. Jack pled guilty to voluntary manslaughter and got three years' probation.

Did Lamson Do It?

On May 30, 1933, the sales manager at Stanford University Press stood in the backyard of his stucco cottage in Palo Alto. The house was located on campus, only "a stone's throw" from the home of former president Herbert Hoover. The publishing official was thirty-one-year-old David Lamson, who wore overalls as he cleaned the yard and burned trash. He spoke with friends who had gathered in the yard and told them he expected a real estate agent to drop by any moment since he and his wife planned to rent out their house while they traveled for the summer.

When the agent arrived at ten o'clock that morning with a potential renter, David entered the house's back door, telling the agent to wait at the front door and he would let them in. He later said that as he walked through the hall to the front door, he noticed his bathrobe and pajamas in the front room and tossed them into the bedroom. Glancing in the bathroom, he saw blood on the floor and his wife Allene, a twenty-eight-year-old campus YWCA secretary, nude and dead in the bathtub, her arms and head hanging over the side.

The people in the yard saw David burst out the front door shouting, "My wife has been murdered!"

Despite having witnesses, David had some explaining to do. He told the police, "I know she was murdered but before God I didn't do it!" Friends of David and Allene were certain she must have slipped in the tub and fractured her skull when her head hit the faucet. However, there were no traces of blood or hair on the tub's fixtures, though there was a pool of blood on the floor and spatters on the walls.

After the autopsy, Undersheriff Earl H. stated that Allene's skull was so badly pulverized with four fractures that it was inconceivable that an ordinary fall could have done such damage. Investigators found bloody garments in the house—not just in the bathroom, as one might expect if Allene had died in an accident, but in three rooms. When police arrived, David's overalls were bloody. Police found a ten-inch section of pipe that had been burned in a fire in the backyard. It was sent out for chemical analysis.

French doors on the couple's patio led to the street. David said one door was open when he found his wife's body. His friends argued that a murderer could have entered the house and bludgeoned Allene as she bathed. If so, however, he must have been a killer of rare nerve, since David was home at the time and talking to friends in the yard; and murder must have been the alleged prowler's only motive since nothing was missing from the cottage. (Early in the investigation, two Stanford students, William P. and John V., made informal statements to the police that they had seen a stranger lurking around the cottage.) If it took courage for a killer to strike while David was at home, it would also have been bold to the point of foolhardiness for David to batter Allene to death while two persons were waiting for him on the front porch and friends were standing in the backyard. The prosecution's theory when David went to trial was that he battered Allene to death early in the morning *before* company arrived, opened the French door to make it look as though there had been an intruder, then pretended to find the body just after the real estate agent arrived at ten o'clock. However, the defense pointed out that the bathtub water and the body were both still warm when investigators arrived.

What about all those bloody clothes? Mrs. Ford B., wife of a Stanford journalism professor, said that she'd entered the bathroom just after David found the body and saw him cradling it. That explains how David got blood on his overalls, argued his staunch friends. David's bathrobe, slippers, pajamas, and two shirts were bloodstained, but Mrs. Ford B. explained that Allene often wore her husband's bathrobe and slippers. David said blood had gotten on the pajamas when he'd entered the house and found them in the front room and carried them into the bathroom. If David had worn one of the shirts while holding his wife's body, that would explain its bloodstains—but how did blood get on the other shirt?

As for the burned pipe in the yard, David said he had no idea how it had gotten there. The State later claimed that chemists found traces of blood on it, and as David had set the bonfire on the morning of his wife's death, if he was innocent the Fates certainly were conspiring most cruelly to make him look as suspicious as possible.

Things appeared bad enough for David that he spent the next night in jail. He went voluntarily, it should be noted, and was not officially booked at that time.

Police photographed the scene with Allene's body *in situ* and decided that she had been struck with a blunt object while standing five feet from the tub and then placed inside it to make it seem as though she'd slipped. The undersheriff announced on June 1 that murder charges would be filed against David.

On June 3, David's attorney, Arthur F., declared that he'd found an *actual eyewitness* to Allene's death. According to Arthur, the unnamed man claimed that he'd surprised Allene while she was bathing, after which she screamed and fell, receiving her fatal injury. The Unknown ran away in fear and was too ashamed to admit what he had done. Arthur would not say whether the witness was a stranger, a friend of the family, or what, only that the man would produce a written statement "at the proper time." But "the proper time" never arrived, and the mysterious witness never came forward, not even when David desperately needed his testimony during his plethora of trials.

On June 19, the judge at the preliminary hearing ruled that the evidence against David, although circumstantial, was compelling and that he must stand trial for murder. Dr. Frederick P., county pathologist, testified that he'd found traces of blood on the burned pipe discovered in the yard and a charred bloody cloth as well. But in a case that has so many infuriating ambiguities, it will not surprise the reader to hear that Dr. Frederick was unable to determine whether the blood on these artifacts was animal or human. (The defense argued that the "bloodstains" on the pipe were in fact vegetable in origin.)

Dr. Frederick did determine that the blood in the house was human and that it was found in some expected places and some surprising locations: on David's pajamas and bathrobe, as the suspect already had admitted, but also on the back porch, under the kitchen doorknob, and on a hallway ceiling trapdoor. Whether he was an innocent man or a diabolically clever killer, it is hard to imagine David incriminating himself by touching so many things with bloody hands.

Dr. Frederick testified that the dead woman's head injuries couldn't have been self-inflicted or accidental but could have been caused by something like the ten-inch pipe found in the bonfire. He added that the blood in the tub's water did not seem fresh. On the other hand, autopsy surgeons testified that the fatal blows could have come from the metal pipe *or* by Allene's striking her head on a curved washbowl in the bathroom.

David's trial began on August 21. The defense made sure the jury included five women, believing they would be sympathetic to their handsome client.

Investigators revealed that David had not slept with his wife the night before her death but rather slept alone in the nursery. David explained at first that she told him she felt sick. But Deputy Sheriff Howard B. testified that as he questioned David, the latter admitted that she was "not really ill." The deputy sheriff thought the nursery bed looked like it was undisturbed, while a pillow on the couch suggested someone had been sleeping on it. Did this hint that the couple had had a marital spat the night before Allene died?

David said he did not know how blood got on his pajamas and bathrobe, claiming that he threw the garments into his bedroom *before* finding the body in the bathroom. (This contradicted what he'd said on the day after Allene's death. Then, David had said the pajamas had become bloodstained when he'd carried them into the bathroom.) Whether the change in his story was wrought by deception, nervousness, or a clearer memory after the fact is a matter of opinion. He also could not explain how one of his slippers came to be found in the hall, stating that he had thrown both in the bathroom.

More trouble for David came during the trial's August 30 session. Friends depicted his marriage as ideal, but one witness testified that David had confessed that his wife was unhappy and that "the situation could not go on indefinitely and that a climax would come soon." (Of course, these words are not necessarily synonymous with "I am planning to commit murder via a pipe over the head.") Evidence indicated that David had been secretly squiring around Sara K., a blond divorcée in Sacramento; the prosecution explained David's roving eye by hinting that

Allene was sexually frigid, a theme they would return to later. The suggestion was that David had slept on a couch (or in the nursery) the night before the murder because she'd rejected his advances by pretending to be sick.

On August 31, Dr. A. W., a Stanford anatomy professor, and county pathologist Dr. Frederick P. testified to the following effect: wounds on Allene's head suggested she had been held by the hair while she received the fatal injuries; spattered blood was found on the bathroom's walls and ceilings, and if she had cracked her head on the faucet the blood would not have traveled so far. If her injuries had been accidental, they would have been possible only if she had fallen twice.

Love poems that Sara had sent to David were duly read aloud in court to the smiles of onlookers. (One started with the line "Life is such fun, dear.") She claimed that she intended them for publication and had wanted his professional literary opinion about them, but oddly the prosecution did not call her in to testify in person.

When the defense got their turn starting September 5, they presented witnesses who had seen David after he found his wife's body and thought he looked "stunned or shocked." Pretty lame—and then things got much worse for David.

On September 7, the judge ruled that the defense could not present testimony arguing that Allene had died an accidental death—a decision the press called "a staggering legal defeat." The defense attorney sputtered that the judge's decision "shut out practically the whole defense," but he was philosophical in the face of crushing ruination: "Our defense is not a theory of accident. It is 'not guilty.' We don't have to prove an accident, but the State must prove it was not an accident, that it was murder and that Dave did it."

The judge's ruling meant that the jury did not get to hear expert testimony from Dr. Charles R., an authority on X-rays who believed Allene had died in an accidental fall. Criminologist George W. believed Allene had indeed struck her head on the washbasin but was not allowed to explain why he thought so.

Perhaps not surprisingly in the face of the judge's refusal to allow David a vigorous defense, on September 16, the jury found him guilty and recommended that he be hanged on December 15. The defense strategy of making sure women were on the jury hadn't helped at all!

The defense attorney vowed that he would file for an appeal immediately and said: "If he hangs, I hope I die before he does. It would kill me anyway. But I reiterate, he will not hang. The record of this case is full of errors." E. O. Heinrich, Berkeley criminologist, called the verdict a "serious miscarriage of justice." Even the deputy sheriff remarked to the prisoner, "You took it on the chin, Dave." David himself declared that he had not lost faith in the American justice system.

Allene's brother Frank T. of Lamar, Missouri, started a court action to gain custody of the couple's daughter, Allene Genevieve, less than three years old.

It certainly looked as though the defense had grounds for an appeal. Twelve days after the verdict, juror Nellie C. complained that the other jurors had bullied and threatened her into voting for first-degree murder. David's attorneys signed an affidavit swearing that juror R. E. G. had not revealed that he was a deputy sheriff and that jury foreman George did not disclose his friendship with Sheriff William E.

After the conviction, a coroners' jury held an inquest. Generally, of course, an inquest is held before a trial, but the prosecution requested that in this case it be delayed until after the trial. They did not explain why. On September 28, the jurors returned an open verdict—a none-too-subtle way of saying they disagreed with the sentence in the case. The jury declared that Allene had died from "violent force applied to the back of the head, resulting in fractures to the skull." But they pointedly did not say David was responsible.

David had the adventure of his life early in the morning of November 27, when a mob broke into the Palo Alto jail with a battering ram and lynched James Holmes and Harold Thurmond, kidnappers and murderers of popular San Jose department store scion Brooke Hart. There was no guarantee the mob would be satisfied with James and Harold, and for a while it was feared they would hang every prisoner in the building, including David. He survived the night and was sent to San Quentin to await a legal hanging.

As David made himself comfortable on Death Row by writing a book about his experiences in that unenviable location, a number of persons agitated for a retrial. Criminologist August V., formerly Berkeley's chief of police, performed a private investigation and announced on February 12, 1934, that he was convinced David was innocent. It appears that the bathroom where Allene had died had not yet been cleaned up; August stated with authority that her cause of death was by falling on a washbowl, adding, "I visited the bathroom and the evidence is still there."

On October 13, the California State Supreme Court ruled that the case against David was "no stronger than mere suspicion" and ordered a second trial. Yet, at the same time, a majority of the justices admitted that they personally thought him guilty. David's brother-in-law Frank welcomed a retrial, saying he thought it would result "only in a more positive conviction."

David's attorneys hoped he would walk out of jail a free man on December 7. Instead, the judge ruled that he must be tried again beginning on February 19, 1935, and refused bail. The very next day, David's seventy-four-year-old mother died in Palo Alto of injuries received in a car crash.

The second trial was well under way when, on March 26, the prosecution presented creative—if not ghoulish—evidence. Dr. Clement A. described a blood spatter experiment he had undertaken using himself as the guinea pig in the interest of science and truth and the pursuit of justice. Specifically, the doctor had allowed someone to cut his throat and slash his head so he could measure the force of arterial blood spurts. (I can think of no parallel to this event in any other murder trial.) The gist of the curious physician's little test was that it was impossible for Allene's blood to have sprayed the walls of the bathroom at a height of six to eight feet if she had been injured in a fall. This medical pioneer is worth quoting:

> I had a doctor cut a lateral and horizontal incision in my neck. It was an inch and a half long cut. He then located the occipital artery in the back of my head and clamped the blood vessel. The arterial blood clamp was suddenly released. The blood spurted only six inches vertically and only eighteen inches laterally.

Not to be outdone, the defense provided a graphic visual aid of their own on April 12, when a bathtub and washbasin were hauled into court and set up exactly as positioned in the bathroom. Christine P., a "pretty brunette" secretary, took a simulated fall into the tub to demonstrate how Allene *could* have died in an accidental fall. The aforementioned Berkeley criminologist Dr. E. O. Heinrich guided the demonstration. (One wonders if David and his defense team were aware that E. O. Heinrich had made a buffoon of himself years earlier during the first trial of film comedian Roscoe Arbuckle, who was unjustly accused of trumped-up charges of rape and manslaughter. The full story of Heinrich's public humiliation when he fobbed himself off as a "fingerprint expert" for the prosecution can be read in David Yallop's book *The Day the Laughter Stopped*.)

A press report noted that "the first experiment was a failure. [Christine], to the amusement of prosecution attorneys, slumped from [E.O.'s] hands as he released her, after lowering her head to the washbasin, and tumbled to the floor, her body entirely out of the tub." The second time, however, it went without a hitch: "[Christine] spun off the washbasin and her body slid downward, half in and half outside the tub. When [E.O.] attempted to lift her, she slid backward into the tub until only her arms and head were projecting. It was in this position [Allene's] body was found."

The jury retired on May 10 to deliberate after a twelve-week trial—very long for the era. On May 12, it was reported that they had still not reached a decision. The jury begged to be dismissed as they were hopelessly deadlocked. The judge refused. The jurors continued their private debate; it was rumored that they were experimenting with falling bodies. On May 14, the jury reported that they were still unable to reach a decision. The judge had mercy and dismissed them. They had remained stuck at a nine-to-three vote after ninety-three hours of deliberation, with the majority in favor of conviction for second-degree murder.

Would there be a third trial? Many thought not, but on May 17, it was announced that David would face a jury again. The prisoner predicted he would be acquitted. The third go-around was declared a mistrial on November 23, on the grounds that two of the 626 persons on the list of jurors could not be located.

It could be fairly argued that by this point the State intended to try David over and over until they got the verdict they wanted.

History repeated itself at the third trial: the jury could not agree, not surprising in a case so full of contradictions and ambiguities. They announced themselves deadlocked on March 23, 1936, after having taken ten ballots, and were dismissed the next day. As at the second trial, they again stalled at a nine-to-three vote in favor of conviction. "Naturally I'm disappointed," said David. "But I'm just as certain as ever that I'll be vindicated finally." Thus far, the murder mystery had cost the state of California an estimated $75,000. David had already spent almost three years in jail, and back to his cell he went.

At last, on April 3, the State decided not to make a fourth attempt. All charges against David were dropped—yet officials made it clear they were not officially exonerating him. His own daughter didn't recognize him when he walked out of court a free man, and he had to be introduced to her. The whole debacle had been, in the words of a reporter, "a community issue and a legal nightmare."

After he regained his freedom, David Lamson expressed a plan to become a writer. The book that he'd occupied himself writing while on Death Row was published as *We Who Are About to Die: Prison as Seen by a Condemned Man* (Scribner's, 1935). Scribner's also published novels by David, and he wrote a number of articles for the *Saturday Evening Post* well into the late 1940s.

And David lost no time getting remarried after his ordeal, this time to Ruth R., a magazine writer he'd met at a Hollywood party in May 1936. He filed for a marriage license on July 22.

It is impossible now to say definitively whether David was guilty of murder or innocent—that he was a victim of circumstances after his wife slipped in the bathtub. A good case could be made for either option. But there is a third possibility that the authorities seemed uninterested in pursuing in their rush to judgment against David: perhaps Allene had been murdered by someone other than her husband, just as he'd suggested right from the start.

Mrs. Phillips Neutralizes a Rival

Mrs. Clara Phillips, a former chorus girl, was jealous; she suspected that Mrs. Alberta Meadows, a comely twenty-year-old widow, was making a play for her husband. On July 12, 1922, Clara lured Alberta into a forest near Los Angeles, smote her head with a hammer, and left the body to the concern of hungry animals and the coroner.

Clara, age twenty-three, was an amateur at this sort of thing. She left an eyewitness—indeed, she was so foolish as to *invite one along*: Mrs. Peggy Caffee, also an ex-chorus girl, who told the police a baroque tale. She had gone on a shopping trip with Clara on the night of July 11, and the seething wife had purchased a hammer. "A girl who works at a bank has been intimate with my husband," she told Peggy, "and I'm going to meet her tomorrow and have a talk with her. Will you come with me?" Much to her later sorrow, Peggy agreed. The next day, Clara and Peggy—after consuming several drinks of whisky—met Alberta at a parking lot. Clara, exuding sweetness and light, asked Alberta if she wouldn't mind giving her a lift in her car, for she so badly wanted to visit her sister!

The unsuspecting Alberta was happy to oblige, and all three women climbed into the car, Clara with a certain hardware implement hidden in her purse. When they got to an appropriately secluded and wooded section at Montecito Heights, Clara asked Alberta to please pull over for a minute. She had something she wanted to tell her.

When the three women stepped out of the car, Clara said to the young widow: "My husband purchased you those tires and that steering wheel." Then she accused Alberta of adultery. Alberta denied the purchase of the automotive parts as well as the more serious accusation, and Clara retorted with a rain of hammer blows, which did not kill the victim as quickly or as neatly as planned. Peggy later testified: "[Alberta] ran down the hill screaming and I ran up the hill screaming." After Peggy ran a certain distance, she heard voices behind her—calm, peaceable voices—the voices of Clara and Alberta, apparently having made up after their little disagreement. Peggy turned around and saw the hammer wielder and her victim walking "arm in arm."

Once they got to the car, however, Clara's tone became accusatory again: "He also bought you that wristwatch." Alberta's denial was greeted with another hammer blow. Alberta ran screaming for help, pursued by Clara, who overtook her and smashed her skull like an eggshell. She didn't stop until Alberta's head and face were pulped. She struck Alberta until the tool broke from the stress—the hammer's head was embedded in the victim's skull. Clara also disemboweled her rival with the hammer's claw end. Still not satisfied, she rolled a stone onto Alberta's body.

During the laborious process described above, Clara turned on Peggy, glared, and said that if she ever ratted her out, she could count on getting the same.

Horrified and nauseated, Peggy fled the scene on foot. Clara picked her up in the victim's car and gave her a ride back to L.A., uttering threats every foot of the way. Peggy maintained her silence out of fear, but the murderer's husband, oil promoter Armour Phillips, felt no need for such discretion. Clara confessed her gruesome crime to him, and the couple drove Alberta's car to Pomona, where they ditched it. After that, Armour informed the sheriff, fearing that his wife was insane and a menace to society. He added that her jealousy was "unwarranted."

The police found out about Peggy and questioned her. She corroborated Armour's story. A few hours later, Clara was arrested in Tucson, Arizona. At first she pretended she was "Mrs. McGuyer" but quickly gave up the charade. A prison matron examined her and found signs of a recent desperate struggle.

When the not-unattractive Clara and a phalanx of detectives arrived in Los Angeles by train on July 16, she subtly expressed her opinion of the news photographers by first smiling and then sticking her tongue out at them. The press retaliated by nicknaming her "The Tiger Woman."

Clara was set to be arraigned on September 18. In the interim, sundry idiots sent her mash notes, boxes of candy, and floral bouquets when what she really needed was a course in anger management. Her attorneys refused to divulge what their line of defense would be. Most trial watchers assumed she would plead insanity, but in October her attorney, Bertram H., hinted that she would plead "the unwritten law"—a defense strategy of shaky legal grounding, often invoked in times past, which held that the despoiler of a person's home pretty well deserved whatever mayhem befell him or her and therefore the defendant should not be held liable for ladling out said mayhem.

Clara's trial began on October 27. Peggy related the events of July 11 and 12 as described above. There wasn't much defense attorney Bertram could do but claim that Clara was a "moron" with "the mind of a child." Also, she had epileptic fits. Also, Bertram implied, she had been drunk at the time. Also, he hinted further, Alberta had started the fight. Also, Clara had undergone a "brainstorm" (that is to say, temporary insanity). Also, Clara was under the influence of Peggy, who, he claimed, had bought the murder weapon and goaded her into fighting. (The more germane question wasn't who *bought* the hammer but rather who employed it to beat out the brains of a fellow human being and then disembowel her.) In modern parlance, it looked very much as if Bertram were determined to fling manure in all directions to see if any of it would stick.

When Clara took the stand on November 2, she—not unexpectedly—told a very different story from Peggy's. As Clara wept and periodically dabbed at her eyes with a handkerchief, she admitted that she had had a fight with Alberta. According to her version of the story, Alberta had confessed her plan to elope with Armour; the aggrieved wife had called her "as dirty as a dog." And then: "She slapped me and we fought, and we fought, and we fought." Just as Alberta was on the verge of winning, Peggy beat her to death with the notorious hammer.

Bertram refused to call Armour to testify. Thus was Armour spared from having to state under oath whether or not he had been having an affair with the victim.

Prosecutor Charles F. forced Clara to admit under oath that she had gotten the story about her husband's having purchased gifts for Alberta from Mrs. Julian M., who had a reputation as a gossip.

On November 9, Mrs. A. W. testified that she had seen Clara—not Peggy—purchase the hammer the day before the murder. This strongly suggested premeditation, not a panicky reaction to getting bested in a fight. According to Mrs. A. W., Clara was so injudicious as to ask the clerk if the hammer was the heaviest one for sale and further inquired: "Do you think this is heavy enough to hit anyone in the head and kill them?" If true, it would be interesting to know what sort of sales pitch the clerk made in reply.

By trial's end, it seemed the best Clara could hope for was a prison term instead of the electric chair. The jury delivered its verdict on November 16: guilty of murder in the second degree, with a sentence of ten years to life in prison. Interestingly, the three women on the jury believed Clara should get death while some of the men wanted to spare her life, perhaps because she was so darn cute; one of them gushed afterward, "She had the most appealing smile I ever saw." The wimpy verdict was settled upon as a compromise. No member of the jury believed the "temporary insanity" defense.

Despite having missed the death penalty by the skin of her beautiful teeth, Clara had the temerity to complain about the sentence: "They didn't give me a fair deal." She had fully expected to be acquitted. Bertram said he would fight till his client was free and announced he would appeal as soon as possible.

Bertram's faith in Clara's innocence must have been shaken by her next action: on the night of December 4, she escaped from her Los Angeles jail cell and disappeared into the healthy California air. She managed to saw through three steel bars, cut out a square of heavy mesh netting, squeeze through the aperture, mince across the jail's rooftop, and ease her way to the ground, where she sped off in a waiting car. Naturally, it was suspected that she had help. Her husband Armour was questioned but claimed he was as baffled as the next guy.

The sheriff had the Mexican border watched, had all depots and major roads out of southern California guarded, and sent bulletins to surrounding towns. But it was too late; the bird had long since flown. Her escape was so well planned that she had six hours of lead time on her pursuers. The only spoor she left behind was a pile of clothes and underwear hidden beneath a building under construction.

Peggy—whom Clara had threatened with death if she ever told what she knew—was so terrified by the news of the escape that she and her husband adopted the pseudonym "Gladson" and considered moving in with her mother in Philadelphia. (The press released these details, apparently not considering that they might be endangering Peggy's life for the sake of a swell story.)

Over the next several weeks, Clara was allegedly seen by nervous people at Tijuana; at the State Fair Grounds in Phoenix, Arizona; on an eastbound train; and in a cabin near L.A. On December 11, a woman who bore a striking resemblance to Clara was arrested in Casper, Wyoming. Striking the resemblance may have been, but she wasn't the Tiger Woman and was released with a contrite apology.

Then, as abruptly as Clara was lost, she was found. On April 21, 1923, the State Department negotiated with the government of Honduras for the extradition of Clara, who had been living in Tegucigalpa. She was arrested at the Hotel Agurcia on

April 24. The authorities refused to take chances this time, even if Clara did have a winning grin that melted the hearts of male jurors. The state of California sent agents to Honduras to personally escort Clara home.

She arrived in New Orleans—along with a cargo of fruit—chained, as any respectable Tiger Woman should be, on May 29. The precautions were wise: Clara was as attractive to Honduran students as she was to American jurors, and fifteen students had been arrested for attempting to spring her out of jail on April 28. The oldest of the badly misguided souls was sixteen.

Still, some people were immune to Clara's charms. As noted, the women on her jury wanted to execute her, and she received little sympathy from the press in an era when female murderers could count on riding waves of sympathy and sentiment unleashed by reporters and columnists. The *Detroit News* remarked: "This is quite unusual. Ordinarily if a woman has brained another with a hammer and thereafter sawed her way out of jail she has every right to expect to have a train of emotional morons on her neck. The more hideous the offense the more marked the phenomenon."

Now that she was back in custody, Clara proved to be as full of hot wind as ever. She claimed she had been framed, that Peggy was the real murderer, and that she had not escaped from jail—she'd been *kidnapped at gunpoint* by Jess Carson, a gun runner and mercenary who'd broken into her cell and insisted that she escape to "right an injustice." Meanwhile, her husband, Armour, nonsensically declared that if Clara was not granted a new trial, he would ask authorities to let him serve the sentence in her place—"even if it means death!"

On June 2, Clara was sent to San Quentin to begin her prison term. She kept quiet until September 1927, when she unsuccessfully attempted suicide by slashing her wrists with broken glass.

In December 1931, Armour Phillips himself was arrested for assault with a deadly weapon. He'd beaten D. J. O'Brien with a blackjack at a Los Angeles party; Armour denied the charge, but officers found the bloody club in his house.

Armour and Clara may have seemed a perfect match for each other—they both had a predilection for beating people with blunt objects—but the bloom was off their romance by June 17, 1935, when Clara was paroled from the State Prison for Women at Tehachapi after serving a paltry twelve years for braining her perceived romantic rival with a hammer and attempting to flee from justice by a sensational escape. Armour had troubles of his own, having been linked to New York gangsters who'd stolen $427,000 from an armored car in August 1934. Armour had promised loudly that when the light of his life was released from prison, he would be the first in line to greet her. Instead he was nowhere to be seen, no doubt afraid to appear in public since he was being sought on a grand theft warrant. Clara was, however, greeted by a crowd who chanted "Tiger Woman, Tiger Woman."

Clara moved to San Diego, where she became a dentist, a fitting trade for one whose luminous beam helped save her from the electric chair. But she was bothered at work by "curious crowds"—one wonders why!—and requested permission to move to her home state of Texas. (She finally moved there in 1961.)

On May 17, 1938, Clara was granted permission to divorce the presumably still-missing Armour. Clara—who had beat another woman to death because she thought she was romantically interested in her husband—now desired to marry another man. Whoever the lucky fellow was, he probably kept her away from the toolbox.

Snake in the Grass; or, The Barbarous Barber

If there was a contest to determine the most unpleasant resident of southern California *ever*, a strong contender would be an inoffensive-looking barber named Robert S. James, formerly of Birmingham, Alabama. Among his qualifications was that he pioneered the use of rattlesnakes as murder weapons.

On August 3, 1935, Robert, age forty-one, reported finding the drowned body of his fifth wife, Mary, an attractive twenty-eight-year-old blonde, in a fishpond at their home. They had been married three weeks. The coroner's jury's verdict was accidental drowning.

However, something about her corpse inspired suspicion—the "something" being that her left foot had puncture marks. Also suspicious was the unseemly zeal with which Robert demanded an immediate payment from his late wife's insurance company. He wanted double indemnity on the grounds that her death was accidental, and a bizarre, outlandish accident at that.

Police suspicions rose higher yet when they found that the red-haired barber had seduced his twenty-one-year-old niece, Lois, who worked as a manicurist in his barber shop; in fact, when he was arrested on a morals charge on April 19, 1936, they were cohabitating.

Then there was Robert's checkered matrimonial history. His first two wives had divorced him. The third had died of natural causes, and the fourth, Winona, had requested an annulment after only one day's marital bliss with him. But she didn't get the annulment fast enough: she was found dead in a bathtub in a Manitou Springs, Colorado, tourist cabin on October 14, 1932. The coroner said she'd drowned. Robert explained that she'd recently been in an auto accident on Pike's Peak that resulted in a fractured skull, and she must have fainted in the bathtub. Why hadn't he taken her to the hospital instead of their cabin? No one seemed to ask, at least not at the time.

On May 2, Charles H. Hope, night manager of a beach café, boasted in a bar that he'd helped murder Mary. The bartender informed the police. When in custody, Charles was overcome with remorse and freely confessed. He had not directly murdered the woman, he said, but he had assisted her killer—her husband, Robert. His statement began:

> The Sunday before they found her dead, I took a box of rattlesnakes I got from [Robert] at Snake Joe's, a snake farm in Pasadena, to [Robert's] house in La Crescenta. That Sunday when I walked into the house at 11 o'clock in the morning, [Robert] had his wife tied with ropes to a breakfast table he had pulled out into the kitchen from the breakfast nook. She had on nothing but a

nightdress, and her eyes and mouth were covered with adhesive tape so she could not see or scream. She was tied down with her body up and her back down against the table.

According to Charles, Robert ordered him: "Go to the garage and get that box of rattlesnakes!" Charles did as he was told and had a front row seat when Robert forced his wife's left foot into the box from which emanated hissing, rattling, and sounds of movement. At least Robert had the common decency to drug her first.

"I know one of them stuck its fangs into her leg," said Charles. "But all the snakes did not rise up and wrap themselves around her. Some of them might have been too old and lazy."

After a while it was evident that the snakes weren't going to feast on Mary as Robert had hoped. The disappointed husband removed her leg from the box and told Charles to take the snakes away. This Charles did, right back to Snake Joe's rattlesnake emporium in Pasadena. One wonders if the next purchaser of the secondhand serpents got a discount.

Charles returned to the residence that night to find Robert in a funk of disgust. "She's not dead yet!" he cried. "This thing's blown higher than a kite. Those snakes were no good. My wife's not even sick. I'm not going to waste any more time. I'm going to drown her." He entered the bathroom while his flunky nursed a whisky in the garage.

At four o'clock that morning, Robert emerged in a triumphant humor. "Well, she's dead now," he said. "I'll clean up the place. Then I'll collect the insurance!" In the wee hours of dawn, Charles helped Robert transport the body to the pond and toss it in.

Conveniently for the police, Robert was already in a Los Angeles cell due to his morals charges against his niece. When told about Charles's confession, he sneered, "You'll find that guy [Charles] will tell you anything. He's screwy!" One can almost visualize the wheels turning in Robert's head; he spent the night of May 2 desperately trying to cook up a story—*any* story—that would shift blame onto Charles and put himself in the best feasible light while explaining away the circumstances of his wife's singularly unpleasant death.

Next morning, Robert admitted that he and Charles had hatched a plot to murder Mary for $21,400 in insurance money, which they planned to split. But, he claimed, his accuser Charles was the actual killer who had held the woman's foot down among the snakes. According to Robert, Charles's original bright ideas were to sprinkle black widow spiders in her bed, or poison her, or perhaps shoot her in a fake holdup. Sure, Robert conceded, his wife had been strapped down to a table, but only so Charles could "perform an illegal operation" (i.e., an abortion) on her. In not so many words, Robert said that he'd gone out for a while, and when he returned home his beloved darling bride was barely alive in bed, butchered by his drunken friend Charles.

According to Robert's version of events, after the bungled abortion, Charles tried to make amends by promising to murder Mary, because that's just the sort of thing true pals do for each other. He forced her foot into the box of snakes. When that proved ineffective, Charles told Robert to go on to his barbershop and spend the day cutting hair, and while Robert was gone Charles would help out his buddy by burning down the house with Mary in it. "But when I came home," said Robert with the attitude of a put-upon victim, "Charles had drowned Mary in the bathtub." "You fool," Robert insisted he'd told Charles, "That's the worst thing you could have done! I had a wife drown in a bathtub in Colorado a little while ago!"

So what else was there to do but toss her body in the pond and make it seem as if she'd drowned there instead?

Police believed none of Robert's nonsense; for one thing, the autopsy on Mary had shown no evidence of a recent abortion. Also, why would he trust his wife's dangerous medical procedure to a man who had already suggested murdering her by poison, gun, or most exotically, by black widow spiders? It was too large a coincidence to swallow that two of Robert's wives had drowned in a bathtub. Like the infamous British murderer George Joseph Smith, who also disposed of his three heavily insured spouses by this method, Robert had attempted the stunt one too many times.

It was up to the courts to decide whether Robert or Charles was solely guilty or whether it was a conspiracy between them. To play it safe, on May 6, a Los Angeles jury indicted both men in what the press called "the rattlesnake death plot."

Investigators looked into Robert's past and turned up much sordidness. Authorities in Manitou Springs, Colorado, investigated the car crash of his fourth wife with renewed interest and found "new peculiar circumstances" surrounding the accident, which may well not have been an accident after all—see below. In any case, she was lavishly insured, and the grieving husband emerged from the tragedy $13,000 richer.

Robert's nephew Cornelius W. had died in a wreck on the highway between San Rafael and Santa Rosa, after which Robert was paid $5,000 on the young man's life, the barber having sagely insured him and named himself the beneficiary. Funny thing was that Robert announced his nephew's death two weeks before it happened—he was so unwise as to make this accurate prediction by sending a telegram to Cornelius's mother, which was gained by investigators—and Charles darkly hinted that someone had tampered with the auto's steering mechanism. Colorado authorities confirmed that the device was "faulty."

Robert's telegram stated that Cornelius's sister Lois was also killed in the wreck. This prediction was untrue; she wasn't even in the car. But perhaps Robert had thought of a better plan for his niece. The reader will recall that he was charged with seducing her. Interestingly, police found that Robert had unsuccessfully tried to take out an insurance policy on her, again naming himself as the beneficiary. Considering his track record, she might have gotten off relatively lucky.

Meanwhile, Charles told anyone who would listen that he was convinced his friend and accomplice Robert had intended to murder him too to get rid of a bothersome witness. Charles recalled that he had become almost fatally sick after drinking some whisky offered to him by Robert and that Robert had been *very* insistent that Charles go for a refreshing swim in the ocean with him. Some inner instinct in Charles—which possibly originated from watching Robert shove a defenseless woman's foot in a box of rattlers—warned him not to go, and he refused each time.

Another surprise emerged when investigators found that Robert had been married a couple more times than anyone knew about. His fifth and final wife was actually his *seventh* and final wife.

Charles pled guilty to first-degree murder. The ex-sailor testified against Robert when the latter went on trial in Los Angeles on June 22, 1936:

> [Robert] lifted her left leg to make room for me to sit the box down on the breakfast nook seat. Suddenly, he grabbed her left leg. He held it over the box. He jerked the top off the box with a quick movement and stuck her foot in it. Her foot was only down there a little while. I heard a rattle and she writhed and threw herself against the straps. She groaned. Then [Robert] took her foot out of the box.

At that point in his testimony, Charles was so overcome with remorse that he got sick and bailiffs led him away from the stand. Robert threw back his head and laughed loudly, a gesture that did little to improve his standing among the jury. Perhaps he was trying to convey an air of "Why, that accusation is so silly that I can't help but chortle!"

On June 28, the prosecution brought into the courtroom glass cases containing two of the notorious rattlesnakes. The record solemnly reveals that their names were Lethal and Lightning. Also present was their owner and snake farm proprietor Joe H., alias "Snake Joe," who testified that they were the very reptiles he'd sold to Charles.

After a five-hour argument between defense and prosecution on July 1, the judge gave the State permission to put up evidence relating to Robert's suspicious past marriages. Thus, on that day, the prosecution put on the stand a man whom Robert was undoubtedly hoping never to see again in his life: J. D. R., superintendent at a Pike's Peak toll road, who contended that back in 1932 Robert had bludgeoned his then-wife Winona with a hammer, stuffed her in their car, then pushed the car over a cliff to simulate a crash. But she survived. Robert was a remarkably incompetent murderer, but what he lacked in skill he made up for in viciousness and persistence. When his plan failed, according to J. D., Robert drove his unconscious wife back to the cabin and drowned her in the bathtub. J. D. had helped recover Winona after her "accident," and he noticed that the back of her head was soft and squishy; that there was a bloody ball peen hammer in the car, which, if Robert had used it as a weapon, he was dumb enough to leave at the scene; and footprints suggesting someone had pushed the car off the ledge. Robert claimed that he had been riding in the car too but had managed to jump out before it went over. J. D. very likely was correct in his suspicions.

On July 3, a young governess, Madge, testified that only a week after Mary had died, the widower was on the prowl to make her his eighth wife. She admitted that they'd spent a week together in a Hermosa Beach hotel, thwarting the suspicions of the hotel dicks by pretending to be man and wife. (Whatever else may be said about Robert, he certainly had a way with women.)

Madge testified, "He said he didn't believe in mourning over the dead and as soon as he buried his wife and collected the insurance he wanted me to marry him and go north." In addition to these sweet nothings, he offered to pay Madge $2,000 if she would falsely testify that she had seen Mary alive and on her porch on the morning she died, complaining that she felt sick. Robert's response, as he had done after his accomplice's damning testimony, was to guffaw heartily as if hoping his ridicule would put reasonable doubt in the jurors' minds.

A moment of low comedy came on July 15 when a herpetologist was performing a scientific test in the courtroom. The rattlesnake known as Lethal got out of his box and slithered toward a crowd of a hundred spectators. There was no "order in the court" that day as shrieking spectators leaped upon tables and chairs. Five minutes of matchless terror dragged by before the herpetologist and "Snake Joe" recaptured Lethal, who had taken refuge under a bookcase. During those five precious minutes of freedom, however, the rattler showed everyone who was boss. Even Robert, who was in the witness chair when the snake got loose, looked pale. Perhaps he wondered what a rattlesnake bite in the leg might feel like.

Several weeks previously, the venom from the rattlesnakes had been tested on two guinea pigs. If Robert had had his way, the poison would have been tested on another guinea pig: himself. On July 16, he offered to stick his foot in the snake cage for the same length of time Charles claimed Mary's foot had been exposed. This, Robert said, would prove "that the snakes would not strike as quickly as [Charles] said and . . . that if they did, the bite would not be serious." The judge refused the offer, stating, "This courtroom is not a three-ring circus. There's been enough sensationalism already." He might have been thinking about Lethal's escape the day before. It would have been interesting to see Robert's reaction if the judge had called his bluff and taken him up on it.

On July 17, the prosecution summed up its case. Robert spent the time ostentatiously reading a book—a San Diego Museum pamphlet on snakes!—perhaps thinking that if loud, inappropriate laughter would not convince a jury of his innocence, a studied air of ennui might. The State's lawyers made darn certain the jury wasn't bored, however, by dumping five rattlesnakes on a table before them. Two were dead and in jars of formaldehyde, but three were alive and entwined like a caduceus—Lethal, Lightning, and their new friend Jimmy. If the State's purpose was to make the jury feel a fraction of the terror Mary must have felt on her final day, mission accomplished!

There wasn't much the defense could say to help their client, and on July 24, the jury found Robert guilty of first-degree murder, for which the death penalty was mandatory. Robert took the news without so much as a blink. "That's that," he said philosophically and redundantly. His penitent stooge Charles received a life sentence.

On July 25, jailors found a razor blade hidden in a mattress in Robert's cell. It had been given to him by some unknown admirer—not one of his fellow prisoners, who so disliked him that they avoided his company and would not speak to him. Nevertheless, somebody out there thought it would be a good idea to let Robert walk the streets free and unencumbered, and on August 12, prison guards found smuggled hacksaws in his cell.

A couple of weeks after his conviction, Robert's attorneys asked for a retrial on the grounds that the jury had been so frightened by the caged snakes on display throughout the trial—not to mention the one that got away, and the wad of living and dead snakes unloaded before the jurors—that it amounted to a prejudicial error. Somebody somewhere disagreed, and the new trial was denied.

On May 1, 1942, after a number of delays that benefited no one but the prisoner, Robert's evil little green eyes were closed forever at San Quentin. Robert had the distinction of being the last man executed by hanging in California, but the honor was somewhat diminished when the rope proved to be the wrong length and he choked slowly for over ten minutes. The world lost a barber that day, but Robert's execution may have saved who knows how many women from having their feet thrust into rattlesnakes, or being drowned in bathtubs, or dying in trumped-up car crashes.

BIBLIOGRAPHY

Baltimore Sun. "Eaten by Red Ants." August 27, 1908, 1.
Bird, Jessica. "Accused Murderess Appears Calm and Unworried at Jail." *Riverside Daily Press.* December 8, 1928, 2.
———. "Mother Intimates Son's Insanity Plea." *Riverside Daily Press.* December 12, 1928, 2.
———. "Northcott Enters Court Room with Apparent Nonchalance and Smiles." *Riverside Daily Press.* January 2, 1929, 2.
Colangelo, Drema. E-mails to author. July 12, 2005; November 13, 2005; November 14, 2005.
Daily Alta California (San Francisco). "To-day's Hanging." October 24, 1884, 5.
Daily Capitol Journal (Salem, OR). "Arrested in Maine for Wife Murder." May 13, 1914, 5.
Duffy, Clinton T. *The San Quentin Story.* Garden City, NY: Doubleday, 1950.
Evening Standard (Ogden, UT). "Author of 'How to Be Happy' Commits Suicide." March 15, 1911, 8.
Holton (KS) Recorder. "How Two Desperadoes Had a Duel All by Themselves." October 3, 1878, 6.
Kansas City Star. "Legends of Ghost Towns Endure in the Old West." January 31, 1954, 77.
———. "Tickets to a Hanging $5." October 19, 1902.
Kokomo (IN) Tribune. "Find Cult Secrets . . ." October 11, 1929, 7.
L.A. Times. "Bizarre Details of Slaying Told." July 24, 1942, I, 10.
———. "Funeral Held for Slain Girl." July 22, 1942, I, 10.
———. "Gireth Asks Press Kindness in Stories of Execution Friday." January 20, 1943, I, 8.
———. "Gireth Dies for Slaying." January 23, 1943, A2.

———. "Gireth Examined by Psychiatrist." July 20, 1942, I, 7.
———. "Gireth Funeral Rites Will Be Private." January 24, 1943, II, 2.
———. "Girl Murder Confessed by Glendale Jeweler." July 18, 1942, I, 7.
———. "Glendale Jeweler Indicted in Auto Court Death of Girl." July 25, 1942, I, 6.
———. "Glendale Jeweler Sentenced to Death in Murder of Girl." August 11, 1942, I, 9.
———. "His Skin Not Bullet-Proof." August 30, 1915, II, 1.
———. "Jealousy Denial Marks Co-ed Slaying Case." July 19, 1942, I, 8.
———. "Jeweler to Plead Insane in Slaying." July 21, 1942, I, 11.
———. "Slaying Case Details Told." July 23, 1942, I, 18.
———. "Wife Pleads for Gireth's Life." January 21, 1943, II, 1.
Louisville Courier-Journal. "$2.20 Murderer Sentenced to Die." January 17, 1931, 2.
———. "3 Killers, Good Friends in Death House . . ." May 23, 1935, 1+.
———. "A Corpse Kept Seven Years." December 23, 1888, 10.
———. "A Dismal 'Third Degree' Fails to Gain Confession." January 26, 1914, 2.
———. "A Duel with Revolvers." September 15, 1878, 1.
———. "A Ghost Photographed." October 18, 1890, 8.
———. "A Los Angeles Inventor Is Reported . . ." November 12, 1915, 2.
———. "A Man Who Eats Mice and Flies." September 8, 1884, 5.
———. "A Race with Death." February 13, 1892, 7.
———. "A Spooky Dinner." Editorial. March 31, 1922, 6.
———. "Accidental Shot Fatal to Columbo." September 3, 1934, 1+.
———. "Alleged Killer Guilty on 3 Morals Counts." May 28, 1936, 13.
———. "An Escort for Corpses." January 10, 1889, 2.
———. "Another Ghoul." November 13, 1878, 3.
———. "Author." March 1, 1935, 8.
———. "Author of Note to Slain Movie Man Identified." July 2, 1938, II, 5.
———. "Barber Announced Nephew Dead Before Fatal Crash . . ." May 9, 1936, 4.
———. "Bath Tub Death Witness Discovered." June 4, 1933, I, 1.
———. "Bequeathed $5 to Buy Book on Wages of Sin." May 30, 1912, 10.
———. "Big-Nose George." March 24, 1881, 3.
———. "Big-Nose George to Be Hanged." December 16, 1880, 3.
———. "Big-Nose George's Crimes." September 15, 1880, 4.
———. "Bill, Who Pulled Frisco Down for Gin Fizz, Dies." November 2, 1933, 4.
———. "Blade of James Is Seized in Cell." July 26, 1936, I, 5.
———. "Body of Boy Tortured Is Found in Bay." July 27, 1933, 1.
———. "Body of Young Woman Thrown from Motor." March 5, 1934, 1.
———. "Bones of Giants Are Unearthed." December 18, 1912, 5.
———. "Boy, 14, Kills His Playmate . . ." August 24, 1939, I, 4.
———. "Boy, 14, Who Slew Playmate Held Insane." September 19, 1939, I, 3.

———. "Boy Faces Jail for False Confession." September 1, 1933, 27.
———. "California Going Mad." April 29, 1888, 17.
———. "Carried Poison Three Years Before Taking It." July 24, 1904, V, 6.
———. "Charge Against Lamson Dropped." April 4, 1936, 1+.
———. "Clara Phillips Gets Freedom Next Year." May 18, 1934, 1.
———. "Clara Phillips Is Behind Prison Bars." June 3, 1923, I, 3.
———. "Clara Phillips Is Nabbed in Honduras." April 25, 1923, 1.
———. "Clara Phillips Is Taken to Castle." May 23, 1923, 1.
———. "Clara Phillips Put on Ship U.S.-Bound." May 28, 1923, 1.
———. "Clara Phillips Says Conviction Framed." May 30, 1923, 3.
———. "Clara Phillips to Disembark Today in New Orleans." May 29, 1923, 1.
———. "Clara Phillips Tries to Kill Self in Jail." September 12, 1927, 5.
———. "Columbo's Family, Gun Owner Friendly." September 4, 1934, 2.
———. "Columbo's Mother Gets 'Son's' Wire." December 23, 1934, I, 7.
———. "Columbo's Mother Still Not Told Her Son Was Killed . . ." September 3, 1939, I, 2.
———. "Convicted Murderer Expects to Get Fun . . . ." June 21, 1935, I, 1+.
———. "Cops Say Boy Admits Mutilation Murder." August 3, 1933, 18.
———. "Cops Sift Past of 'Snake' Man." May 8, 1936, III, 10.
———. "Couple Dies in Suicide Pact . . ." June 14, 1938, I, 8.
———. "Court Hears Plan to Sell 'Petrified' Body." December 20, 1928, 3.
———. "Criminologist Says Lamson Is Innocent." February 13, 1934, 2.
———. "Crooner's Death Kept from Mother 3 Years." December 14, 1936, II, 8.
———. "Cult Cemetery Hunt Continues." October 14, 1929, 3.
———. "Cult's High Priestess Convicted of Theft." March 3, 1930, 1+.
———. "David Lamson to Wed Magazine Writer." July 23, 1936, 1.
———. "Death Given in Snake Murder." July 25, 1936, 1+.
———. "Defense Rests in Hammer Murder Trial." November 19, 1922, 3.
———. "Diagram Shows in Detail How Mrs. Clara Phillips, Hammer Murderer, Escaped." December 16, 1922, 5.
———. "Doctor Lets Own Throat Be Cut . . ." March 27, 1935, I, 1.
———. "Eagan Plays Jazz, Drinks Before Death." October 21, 1933, 1.
———. "Escorts Arrive to Fetch Mrs. Phillips." May 19, 1923, 5.
———. "Executed in Cheerful Mood." June 22, 1935, 14.
———. "Execution of Indian Bungled." July 14, 1936, 2.
———. "Fourth Lamson Jury Says It's Deadlocked." March 24, 1936, 1.
———. "Free Again." June 18, 1935, 7.
———. "Garrison Sues Cops for $50,000." August 14, 1931, 13.
———. "Garrison's Threats Bared." July 25, 1931, 1.
———. "Ghost Stories." January 18, 1885, 14.
———. "Ghouls Enter Tomb of Dead Gypsy King." May 31, 1924, 3.
———. "Girl, 22, Is Found Hanged on Tree." April 20, 1931, 1.
———. "Girl, 22, Found Stabbed to Death." May 4, 1931, 1+.

———. "Girl Drives Nail in Head." February 24, 1937, I, 10.
———. "Girl Falls into Bathtub in Court . . ." April 13, 1935, 1.
———. "Girl Found Hanged Battled Assailant." April 21, 1931, 1.
———. "Girl Loses Arm to Follow Impulse." September 7, 1930, I, 6.
———. "Girl Is Slain, Fiend Sought." August 19, 1934, I, 1+.
———. "Girl's Friend Is Arrested for Murder." May 12, 1931, 1.
———. "Girl's Slayer Given Life Term in Prison." September 18, 1934, 3.
———. "Grave Diggers Make Trouble." June 9, 1903, 11.
———. "Grondin Acquitted of Wife-Murder Charge." February 7, 1914, 6.
———. "Gun That Killed Cameraman Found in Vacant Lot." July 8, 1938, I, 18.
———. "Hammer Murder Law Fight Near." October 21, 1922, 14.
———. "Hammer Murder Net Is Tightened." July 16, 1922, I, 1+.
———. "Hammer Murder Story Is Upset." November 10, 1922, 3.
———. "Hammer Murder Trial Date Set." July 21, 1922, 3.
———. "Hammer Murderer's Husband Held." December 28, 1931, 12.
———. "Hammer Slayer Denies Breaking Jail; Was Kidnapped, She Says." May 31, 1923, 1.
———. "Hammer Victim and Witness." July 20, 1922, 5.
———. "Hanged by a Single Hair." November 16, 1884, 4.
———. "He Wanted to Jump." February 15, 1886, 5.
———. "Hollywood Gun Victim Gambler." December 29, 1938, II, 2.
———. "Husband of Woman . . ." June 1, 1933, 1.
———. "Husband on Trial in Wife's Death Monday." August 20, 1933, I, 2.
———. "Indians Bury Victim of Smallpox Alive." March 13, 1921, I, 1.
———. "Indian, Eager to Hang, Says Judge Is Liar." June 18, 1936, 16.
———. "Indian Is Hanged After Three-Hour Band Concert." November 30. 1912, 4.
———. "Inquest in Lamson Case Aids Defense." September 29, 1933, 14.
———. "James' Aide Gets Life in Wife Murder Case." July 29, 1936, 12.
———. "James Reads Book at Trial." July 18, 1936, 10.
———. "Judge Deals Blow to Lamson Defense." September 8, 1933, 7.
———. "Judge to Instruct Phillips Jury Today." November 15, 1922, 5.
———. "Judge Refuses James' Offer to Expose Himself to Snakes." July 17, 1936, 14.
———. "Jury Gives Lamson Death for Murdering Wife." September 17, 1933, I, 1+.
———. "Jury Report Stuns Lamson." March 26, 1936, 4.
———. "Jury Still Out in Wife-Murder Trial." May 12, 1935, I, 1.
———. "Keeps Daughter's Body Twenty-Seven Years." December 2, 1905, 6.
———. "Keeps Sister's Death Secret." February 1, 1914, I, 2.
———. "Kidnapper of 2 Texas Cops Dies on Gallows." June 20, 1936, 2.
———. "Kissing Dead Man Causes Wife's Illness." July 11, 1936, 7.
———. "Lamson Faces Murder Trial." June 20, 1933, 1+.
———. "Lamson Gets New Trial in Wife's Death." October 14, 1934, I, 1+.

———. "Lamson in Death Cell." October 7, 1933, 16.
———. "Lamson Juror Charges Coercion." September 12, 1933, 8.
———. "Lamson Jurors Fail to Agree." March 25, 1936, 3.
———. "Lamson Jury Retires for Fourth Night." May 14, 1935, 1.
———. "Lamson Looked 'Stunned.'" September 6, 1933, 5.
———. "Lamson May Claim Mishap Killed Wife." August 26, 1933, 1.
———. "Lamson Must Face Trial, Court Rules." December 8, 1934, 8.
———. "Lamson Plans Fight for Life." September 18, 1933, 1.
———. "Lamson Will Face Charge of Murder." June 2, 1933, 10.
———. "Lamson's Mother Dies of Crash Hurts." December 9, 1934, I, 12.
———. "Lamson's Third Hearing Mistrial." November 24, 1935, I, 3.
———. "Lethal Gas Used in First 'Trailer Suicide.'" September 6, 1937, II, 3.
———. "Little Hope Seen for Verdict . . ." May 13, 1935, 1+.
———. "Loose Snake Panics Trial." July 16, 1936, 1+.
———. "Lost His Life on a Poker Bet." February 10, 1896, 13.
———. "Man Admits He Killed Girl, 8." July 14, 1934, 1+.
———. "Man Admits He Slew Young Mother for $2." November 6, 1930, 1.
———. "Man to Be Tried in San Diego Death." June 12, 1931, 15.
———. "Man in Best Suit Blasts Self to Death." November 19, 1937, I, 1.
———. "Man Describes Snake Slaying." June 26, 1936, III, 2.
———. "Man Ends His Life in Electric Chair." February 27, 1929, 1.
———. "Man Facing Doom Nibbles Orange." February 15, 1925, I, 1.
———. "Man Free in Death of San Diego Girl." August 1, 1931, 1.
———. "Man Kills Wife, Self in Lethal Gas Chamber." April 6, 1937, I, 4.
———. "Man Kills Self at Bier of Another." October 5, 1923, 4.
———. "Man Lavishes Money 11 Years on Burial Plot Then Dies Pauper." March 19, 1922, I, 1.
———. "Man Puts His Head on Rail, Train Cuts It Off." January 10, 1933, 3.
———. "Man Puts Radio on Casket for His Soul." July 19, 1925, V, 3.
———. "Man Who Slew So He Could Die Faces Life Term." November 14, 1939, I, 7.
———. "Man Whose Snake-Bitten Wife Found Drowned . . ." May 3, 1936, I, 13.
———. "Man's Suicide Plan Fails but Blast Kills Him." July 12, 1938, I, 3.
———. "Mate Held with Wife in Hammer Slaying." October 13, 1922, 5.
———. "Message to Parents Written by Slayer." June 23, 1935, I, 3.
———. "Mother Sells Nooses to Save Condemned Son." April 4, 1936, 9.
———. "Mothers Testify in Boy Slaying." August 26, 1939, II, 1.
———. "Mrs. Phillips, Guilty of Hammer Murder, Fights for Freedom." November 17, 1922, 1.
———. "Mrs. Phillips Is Firm in Grilling." November 4, 1922, 2.
———. "Mrs. Phillips May Escape Again, Fear." April 27, 1923, 7.
———. "Mrs. Phillips' Plot to Escape Nipped." May 2, 1923, 12.
———. "Mrs. Phillips Seen at Tijuana, Report." December 8, 1922, 11.
———. "Mrs. Phillips Sees Relatives in Texas." June 1, 1923, 1.

———. "Mrs. Phillips to Return in Irons." May 6, 1923, VII, 4.
———. "Murder Seen as Movie Man Shot to Death." July 1, 1938, I, 18.
———. "Murdered a Man for Twenty-Five Cents." February 1, 1902, 10.
———. "Mutilation Story Revealed as Hoax." August 5, 1933, 1.
———. "Musty Trunk Echoes Sealed-Tomb Mystery." Magazine. December 1, 1935, 3.
———. "'Mystery Woman' Takes Her Life." April 30, 1933, I, 6.
———. "New Trial Sought in Rattlesnake Case." August 9, 1936, I, 1.
———. "Ninety-One-Year-Old Hermit Won't Need a Tomb . . ." November 20, 1925, 2.
———. "Nugget in Human Skull." October 29, 1939, I, 13.
———. "Odor of Violets Makes Rift in Clouded Mind." February 2, 1914, 5.
———. "One of the Last Requests of Willard Shannon . . ." June 24, 1928, III, 9.
———. "Parrot to Rest with Dead Woman." May 14, 1933, I, 3.
———. "Party Attended by Slain Movie Man Probed." July 3, 1938, I, 4.
———. "Phillips Cabin First Real Clew in Escape." January 2, 1923, 1.
———. "Phillips 'Ignorant' of Mate's Escape from Los Angeles Lockup." December 6, 1922, 1.
———. "Phillips Linked to Gangsters." August 25, 1934, 2.
———. "Pinioned by Rock, Miner Starves to Death." October 31, 1911, 4.
———. "Pitiful Death Story of Imprisoned Miner." November 1, 1911, 1.
———. "Planes Hunt Mrs. Phillips Along Border." December 7, 1922, 1.
———. "Plot to Kill with Spiders Is Charged." May 4, 1936, 1+.
———. "Poems Read in Lamson's Trial." September 1, 1933, 11.
———. "Prison Guard Electrocutes Self 'By Mistake.'" May 21, 1939, I, 13.
———. "Prison Warden Cruel, Is Charge." December 14, 1924, I, 8.
———. "Promises a Visit from Spirit Land." March 11, 1904, 1.
———. "Proposal No. 8 Told at Trial." July 4, 1936, 18.
———. "Prosecution Sift Sought." August 2, 1931, I, 3.
———. "Queerest Family in the World." May 5, 1907, I, 9.
———. "Recluse Gave $300 for Kiss, Kin Asserts." December 27, 1933, 1.
———. "Red-Haired Uxoricide Hears Sentence Calmly." September 11, 1936, I, 2.
———. "Reporter Writes 'Copy' of His Proposed Suicide." September 21, 1916, 7.
———. "Russ Columbo's Mother Still Kept in Ignorance of Death." July 2, 1938, I, 8.
———. "Saws Sent James." August 13, 1936, 12.
———. "Science Called in Lamson Case." February 18, 1935, 3.
———. "Second Lamson Jury Fails to Reach Verdict." May 15, 1935, 1.
———. "Second Murder Laid to Barber." July 2, 1936, 10.
———. "Sheriff Says Jealous Woman May Have Hanged Girl to Tree." April 22, 1931, 1+.
———. "Slain Capitalist Found in Cellar." September 24, 1920, 1.
———. "Slain Girl's Admirer Indemnified." May 7, 1931, 4.

———. "Slain Movie Man Thought Holdup Victim." July 4, 1938, I, 5.
———. "Slayer Denied Request to Die with Friends." May 24, 1935, I, 1.
———. "Slayer Wants to Move." August 20, 1936, 22.
———. "Snakes Put on Call as Court Exhibits." June 29, 1936, 14.
———. "Sob Sisters Not with Her." May 10, 1923, 6.
———. "Stolen from the Grave." November 2, 1879, 2.
———. "The Strange Possible Complications of Marrying a Twin." Magazine. March 25, 1923, 4.
———. "Strife in Lamson Home Is Charged." August 31, 1933, 1.
———. "Suicide Attempt Cures Paralytic." August 6, 1929, 3.
———. "Suicide Hurries to Save Insurance." October 6, 1933, 29.
———. "Suicide's Heart Left to Doctor . . ." June 12, 1933, 2.
———. "Suspect Views Body of Slain Ex-Fiancée." May 5, 1931, 1.
———. "Third Lamson Jury Is Locked Up for Night." March 22, 1936, I, 18.
———. "Third Murder Trial Ordered for Lamson." May 18, 1935, 4.
———. "Three-Day Funeral Ends with Concert." May 5, 1933, III, 9.
———. "Tom Salmon's Last Words." January 28, 1899, 3.
———. "Treasure Hunt Ends with Finding of Body." February 2, 1935, 1.
———. "Two Are Indicted in Snake Death Plot." May 7, 1936, 1.
———. "Two Boys Trap Murder Suspect." July 28, 1933, 24.
———. "U.S. Going After Hammer Suspect." April 22, 1923, I, 9.
———. "U.S. Police to Go for Mrs. Phillips." May 1, 1923, 1.
———. "U.S. Seaman Jokes as He Kills Himself." June 4, 1937, I, 1.
———. "Warden Bans Blind Man from Sensing Execution." September 30, 1939, I, 3.
———. "'Warm' Clew Found in Hammer Slayer Pursuit." December 9, 1922, 11.
———. "Widow, 20, Slain; Irate Wife Held." July 15, 1922, 1+.
———. "Wife Killer Driven by Remorse to Suicide." January 3, 1939, I, 3.
———. "Wife Slayer Writes Note on Body." August 26, 1938, I, 12.
———. "Wild Waves." November 22, 1922, 6.
———. "Witness Details Hammer Murder." October 28, 1922, 2.
———. "Woman Arrested May Be Hammer Slayer." December 12, 1922, 1.
———. "Woman Held at Casper, Wyo., Not Mrs. Phillips." December 13, 1922, 2.
———. "Woman Held Guilty in Fraud Faces 25 Years." December 23, 1928, I, 9.
———. "Woman Held in Hammer Murder Is Said to Have Mind of Child." November 1, 1922, 15.
———. "Woman Mutilated While Still Alive." October 20, 1933, 22.
———. "Woman Now on Trial in Hammer Murder Accuses 'Eyewitness.'" November 3, 1922, 1+.
———. "Woman Slain After Telling of 'Hunch.'" March 27, 1938, I, 4.
———. "Woman Who Slew Rival to Remarry." May 18, 1938, I, 10.
———. "Woman with Phobia for Hiding Believed Exposure Victim." June 22, 1937, I, 8.

———. "Woman's Body Found in Bags." October 16, 1933, 1.
———. "Women at a Grave." August 17, 1879, 1.
———. "Women Meet in Hammer Murder." July 17, 1922, 1+.
———. "Youth Says He Slew Girl in San Diego." October 2, 1931, I, 1+.
Maurer, Mary. "The Moon Mystery." *Caddo—My Home Town*. July 2007. http://mem55.typepad.com/caddo_my_home_town/2007/08/index.html.
Morning Oregonian (Portland). "Kept Dead Body in House." November 28, 1905.
Nash, Jay Robert. *Encyclopedia of World Crime*. Wilmette, IL: Crime-Books Inc., 1990.
National Police Gazette. "The Loves of Lipsis." August 30, 1879, 3.
Nevada State Journal (Reno). "Parrot Chloroformed at Owner's Request." May 14, 1933, 1.
New Orleans Times-Picayune. "Chicken Feast Before Hanging." December 7, 1912, 7.
New York Times. "Arraign Northcott Quickly for Murder." December 1, 1928, 36.
———. "Bones Are Found at 'Murder Farm.'" September 18, 1928, 16.
———. "California Mob Demands to 'See' Northcott . . ." February 11, 1929, 10.
———. "Indict Northcotts in Farm Murders." September 22, 1928, 21.
———. "Man Leaves His Property to a Deaf and Dumb Asylum . . ." November 17, 1871, 1.
———. "Moves to Get Northcotts." September 25, 1928, 9.
———. "Northcott Admits One Ranch Murder." November 30, 1928, 25.
———. "Northcott Convicted of Slaying 3 Boys . . ." February 8, 1929, 1.
———. "Northcott Enters Plea of Not Guilty." December 5, 1928, 9.
———. "Northcott Has 'Nerves.'" January 14, 1929, 14.
———. "Northcott Indicted in Los Angeles." October 4, 1928, 10.
———. "Northcott Is Sentenced." February 12, 1929, 22.
———. "Northcott Is Taken in Farm Murders." September 20, 1928, 31.
———. "Northcott Jeers Captors." February 9, 1929, 9.
———. "Northcott to Confess." January 2, 1929, 13.
———. "Orders Extradition of Northcott." November 8, 1928, 5.
———. "Says He Aided Northcott." January 15, 1929, 20.
———. "Seized Woman Admits She Is Mrs. Northcott." September 21, 1928, 60.
———. "Story of Four Slain on Farm Is Doubted." September 16, 1928, I, 20.
———. "To Test Sanity of Northcott." January 5, 1929, 6.
———. "Upholds Boy's Tale of 'Murder Farm.'" September 17, 1928, 16.
———. "Warrants Issued in Farm Murders." September 19, 1928, 31.
O'Brien, Robert. "An Interview with Leslie Gireth . . ." *San Francisco Chronicle*. July 19, 1942, 1+.

"People v. Stearns (1973) 35 CA3d 304." *Justia.com*. August 25, 2014. http://law.justia.com/cases/california/calapp3d/35/304.html.

Philadelphia Times. "A Stage Manager's Suicide." May 5, 1879, 1.

The Poke. "This Obituary from 1854 Features the Worst Possible Way to Die." 2013. www.thepoke.co.uk/2016/09/12/obituary-1854-features-worst-possible-way-die/.

Richmond (KY) Register. "Party Incident No Prank; Death Uninvited Guest." October 3. 1967.

Riverside (CA) Daily Press. "Accused Man Fails as Guide." December 5, 1928, 4+.

———. "Add Evidence in Northcott Case." October 4, 1928, 2.

———. "Alleged Confession Excites Northcott." January 25, 1929, 2.

———. "Another Boy Witness in Northcott Case." February 1, 1929, 2.

———. "Another Missing Lad Being Traced." October 17, 1928, 2.

———. "Arraignment of Northcotts Plan." December 10, 1928, 11.

———. "Asserted Slayer Cannot Escape Trial for Murder." January 10, 1929, 1.

———. "Await Coming of Important Witness." October 9, 1928, 2.

———. "'Black Hand' Now Injected into Case." October 13, 1928, 2.

———. "Chemists' Findings Reveal Soil Stained with Human Blood." September 19, 1928, 2.

———. "Child Slayer Collapses as Death Hovers." October 2, 1930, 1.

———. "Court Denies Defense Move Change of Venue." January 8, 1929, 1+.

———. "Cyrus Northcott Promises Truth." December 6, 1928, 2.

———. "'Daddy' Northcott Called to Stand." January 29, 1929, 11.

———. "Death on Gallows Awaits Young Northcott." February 11, 1929, 2.

———. "Defense Wants Mrs. Northcott." January 4, 1929, 2.

———. "Detectives Busy in Northcott Case." September 28, 1928, 2.

———. "Discredit Story of Finding Boys." November 16, 1928, 9.

———. "District Attorney Instructed to Act in Affidavit Matter." January 25, 1929, 2.

———. "Dragging Sump-Hole for More Evidence." September 25, 1928, 2.

———. "Entire Jury Panel Challenged by Defense . . ." January 3, 1929, 1+.

———. "Evidence of Gruesome Murders Uncovered . . ." September 15, 1928, 2.

———. "Evidence Points to Missing Boys." October 6, 1928, 11.

———. "Examination of Northcott Next." December 5, 1928, 2.

———. "Extradition Papers in Northcott Case Must Be Modified." September 26, 1928, 2.

———. "Fails to Break Down Testimony Clark Boy." January 17, 1929, 2.

———. "Fight Is on to Save Northcott from Punishment." September 21, 1928, 6.

———. "First Witness in Northcott Case May Be Called Today." January 9, 1929, 2.

———. "Fourth Victim Northcott." September 24, 1928, 2.
———. "Glenavon Lad Long Missing." October 12, 1928, 15.
———. "Gordon Stewart Northcott Must Pay for His Crimes on Gallows." February 8, 1929, 1.
———. "Grand Jury Acts in Northcott Case." September 21, 1928, 6.
———. "Hard Row Ahead for Northcott." January 19, 1929, 2.
———. "'If the Boy Hangs I'll Die' Says Mrs. Louise Northcott." January 1, 1929, 2.
———. "Informant Says Saw Northcott." December 7, 1928, 2.
———. "Irregularity in Order for a Commission." January 4, 1929, 1+.
———. "Jury Will Get Case Tomorrow." February 6, 1929, 2.
———. "L.A. Grand Jury Indicts Northcott." October 3, 1928, 2.
———. "Lad Identifies Young Northcott." January 4, 1929, 2.
———. "Lad Queried; Sticks to Story." December 1, 1928, 2.
———. "Life Was Too Hard for Composer's Son." December 19, 1928, 1.
———. "Location of Girl Kept a Deep Secret." October 18, 1928, 12.
———. "Louise Northcott Is Mother of Stewart." November 30, 1928, 2.
———. "Louise Northcott Too Late to Go on Stand This Morning." January 28, 1929, 2.
———. "Map Located in Northcott Home." December 6, 1928, 2.
———. "May Extradite Northcott Soon." November 6, 1928, 2.
———. "Men and Women Strain Barriers to Hear Trial." January 21, 1929, 2.
———. "Mother Would Help Her Son." January 3, 1929, 1+.
———. "Mother's Absence Disappoints Youth." January 28, 1929, 2.
———. "Mrs. Northcott Confesses Killing." December 31, 1928, 1+.
———. "Mrs. Northcott Reaches Riverside." December 8, 1928, 2.
———. "Murder Case May Go to Jury Friday." February 2, 1929, 10.
———. "Near Victim on Witness Stand." January 18, 1929, 2.
———. "No Murder Done on Chicken Farm." January 31, 1929, 2.
———. "Northcott Waits Impending Doom." October 1, 1930, 4.
———. "Northcott Cannot See Any Reporters." September 22, 1928, 2.
———. "Northcott Case Expense Shared." October 24, 1928, 11.
———. "Northcott Denies He Confessed." November 30, 1928, 1+.
———. "Northcott Did Not Like to Be Arrested Again." September 28, 1928, 1.
———. "Northcott Has His Raven-Black Locks Trimmed by Barber." January 19, 1929, 2.
———. "Northcott Here for January 2 Trial . . ." December 5, 1928, 4.
———. "Northcott His Own Attorney." January 16, 1929, 2.
———. "Northcott Hits at Newspapers." February 5, 1929, 2.
———. "Northcott Is 'Highhatting' This Country." December 1, 1928, 1.
———. "Northcott Is Under Guard." September 20, 1928, 1+.
———. "Northcott Issues Denial Statement." September 24, 1928, 2.
———. "Northcott Jury Visits at Ranch." January 26, 1929, 11.

———. "Northcott Led into Court by Two Deputies." January 22, 1929, 4.

———. "Northcott Makes Strange Assertion of Relationship." January 22, 1929, 4.

———. "Northcott May Be Sent South Today." November 26, 1928, 4.

———. "Northcott Must Be Own Lawyer." January 24, 1929, 2.

———. "Northcott Offers to Plead Guilty." October 26, 1928, 11.

———. "Northcott Pleads Illness in Court." January 21, 1929, 2.

———. "Northcott Pleads Not Guilty on Three Charges of Murder." December 4, 1928, 2.

———. "Northcott Talks to Save His Life." February 7, 1929, 2.

———. "Northcott Trial in Los Angeles." October 23, 1928, 2.

———. "Northcott Will Ask for Counsel." January 23, 1929, 12.

———. "Northcott's Father Breaks Under Grill of Police Officers." September 17, 1928, 2.

———. "Northcott's Map Is Received Here." October 4, 1930, 2.

———. "Northcott's Mother to Be Brought Back from San Quentin." January 15, 1929, 2.

———. "Northcotts Plead Not Guilty to Murder of Walter Collins." December 12, 1928, 2.

———. "Northcotts Shy at One Name in Case." February 4, 1929, 2.

———. "Northcotts Still Held Prisoners." September 27, 1928, 2.

———. "No Word Received from Officers in North . . ." October 16, 1928, 1.

———. "Other Inmates of the Jail Watching Him . . ." January 3, 1929, 2.

———. "Priest Goes on Stand in Trial Today." January 11, 1929, 1+.

———. "Sanford Clark and Sister Jessie in Pathetic Meeting Here Saturday." October 22, 1928, 2.

———. "Says Northcott Slayer of Boys." January 15, 1929, 2.

———. "Scouts Confession Left by Northcott." October 2, 1930, 2.

———. "Search Ends as Sister Is Found Alive." September 21, 1928, 1+.

———. "Search for Bodies Proves Unavailing." October 3, 1930, 14.

———. "Search for Earth of Northcott Ranch." October 5, 1928, 2.

———. "Secret Kept in Gallows Shadow." October 2, 1930, 1.

———. "Sending Affidavit on Mrs. Northcott." October 15, 1928, 2.

———. "Shocking Narrative Unfolded on Stand." January 30, 1929, 2.

———. "Take Northcott to Murder Farm." December 3, 1928, 2.

———. "To Claim Blood Spots His Own." January 17, 1929, 2.

———. "Two Scientists for Commission in Murder Case." January 5, 1929, 2.

———. "Want Northcott to Point Out Graves." February 11, 1929, 2.

———. "Warrants Issued for Arrest of Young Northcott and His Mother." September 18, 1928, 2.

———. "Will Seek to Have Annulled Sentence of Mrs. Northcott." January 16, 1929, 2.

———. "Winnifred Clark Denies Northcott Is Her Own Child." February 1, 1929, 2.

———. "Winslow Murder Case Up Monday." January 12, 1929, 10.

———. "Young Informant 'Mugged' at Jail." September 28, 1928, 2.

Rix, George. "Northcott's Indifference Overcome by Young Clark's Damaging Recital." *Riverside Daily Press*. January 15, 1929, 6.

———. "Pencil Sketch of Dapper Youth on Trial . . ." *Riverside Daily Press*. January 10, 1929, 4.

———. "Personal Impression of Accused Slayer." *Riverside Daily Press*. December 5, 1928, 4.

———. "Woman Caught in Time's Whirlpool." *Riverside Daily Press*. December 13, 1928, 11.

Rogers, Ben to J. B. Parkes. March 15, 1876. Parkes Family Series, Watts Family Papers, Special Collections and Archives, Crabbe Library, Eastern Kentucky University.

Rogers, Ben to J. B. Parkes. April 17, 1876. Parkes Family Series, Watts Family Papers, Special Collections and Archives, Crabbe Library, Eastern Kentucky University.

San Bernardino County Sun. "Murder Plot." November 6, 1930, 1.

San Francisco Call. "The Man with a Wooden Family." Magazine. October 21, 1906, 1+.

San Francisco Chronicle. "A Mad Maniac's Fate." January 18, 1892, 1.

———. "Carnation Killer, Leslie B. Gireth Sentenced to Die in Gas Chamber." August 11, 1942, 7.

———. "Carnation Killing." July 20, 1942, 5.

———. "Crime Report." July 24, 1942, 13.

———. "The Execution of Gireth." January 23, 1943, 9.

———. "Gireth Admits Guilt Before Grand Jury." July 25, 1942, 9.

———. "Gireth Calm in Court Appearance." July 21, 1942, 5.

———. "Gireth Now Is Ready For 'His Medicine.'" July 22, 1942, 4.

———. "Gireth Pleads Guilty." August 5, 1942, 7.

———. "Gireth Pleads Guilty in Killing." August 5, 1942, I, 5.

———. "Gireth Wins Continuance of One Week . . ." July 29, 1942, 13.

———. "Gireth Won't Talk . . ." January 20, 1943, 7.

———. "Leslie Gireth's Dilemma . . ." July 23, 1942, 11.

———. "Leslie Gireth, Wife Asks Stay of Execution . . ." January 21, 1943, 13.

———. "Noe Valley Spooks." December 24, 1884, 3.

———. "Slayer Strews Flowers at Bedside." July 18, 1942, 1.

———. "Warren Won't Intervene . . ." January 22, 1943, 11.

San Francisco Examiner. "Sits on Hot Stove to Avoid Evil Spirits." October 11, 1904, 5.

"San Francisco Items." *Sacramento Daily Union*. January 13, 1854, 2.

San Jose Evening News. "A Large Gift to Stanford." February 16, 1899, 4.

Santa Cruz Sentinel. "Folsom Prison Guard Dies in Showoff Stunt." May 20, 1939, 8.

Van Nuys News. "Accused Denies Committing Murder at Halloween Party." September 18, 1969, B1.

———. "Investigate Fatal Shooting at Valley Halloween Party." October 31, 1967, A1.

———. "Jurors to Resume Deliberations on Halloween Murder." September 23, 1969, A5.

———. "Jury Begins in 1967 Slaying Case." August 26, 1969, A16.

———. "Man Handed Life Term for Murder." October 31, 1969, A7.

———. "Racket Link Charged at Death Trial." September 14, 1969, A8.

———. "Trial Continues in Halloween Killing." August 17, 1969, A12.

———. "Witness Identifies Defendant in Halloween Slaying Trial." September 4, 1969, A29.

Wallis, Charles L. *Stories in Stone*. New York: Oxford University Press, 1954.

Williams, Brad, and Choral Pepper. *The Mysterious West*. Cleveland: World Publishing Co., 1967.

Wolf, Marvin J., and Katherine Mader. *Fallen Angels*. New York: Ballantine, 1986.

Yallop, David. *The Day the Laughter Stopped*. New York: St. Martin's, 1976.

KEVEN MCQUEEN IS AN INSTRUCTOR IN THE DEPARTMENT of English at Eastern Kentucky University. He is the author of numerous books, including *The Kentucky Book of the Dead*, *Murder and Mayhem in Indiana*, and *The Axman Came from Hell and Other Southern True Crime Stories*.

www.ingramcontent.com/pod-product-compliance
Lightning Source LLC
Chambersburg PA
CBHW020937090426
42736CB00010B/1172